Music,
My Love

Music, My Love

Jean-Pierre Rampal
An Autobiography with Deborah Wise

RANDOM HOUSE
NEW YORK

Library of Congress Cataloging-in-Publication Data
Rampal, Jean-Pierre.
Music, My Love
1. Rampal, Jean-Pierre.   2. Flute-players—France—
Biography.   I. Wise, Deborah.   II. Title.
ML419.R33A3   1989   788'.51'0924 [B]   88-43171
ISBN 0-394-56578-9

Manufactured in the United States of America
24689753
First Edition

Deborah Wise would like to thank Steven Levy for suggesting this book, and Joane Bennett, who helped her understand the flute.

To my mother, who gave me life
To my father, who taught me its meaning
To my wife, Françoise, who makes it so beautiful

Contents

Introduction

I'VE PROBABLY PLAYED THE Mozart G-major Flute Concerto in every country in the world that can provide an orchestral accompaniment. The concerto is like an old friend who becomes dearer and closer with every meeting; sometimes you are surprised by a new opinion, other times just delighted to hear the same old stories told again and again.

Forty years ago, at the start of my professional music career, playing a flute concerto as a visiting soloist with a major symphony orchestra would have been inconceivable. A flute concerto belonged to the first-chair flutist in the orchestra. Much has changed since then, and I won't deny I have played a part in these changes. Perhaps to the chagrin of a few orchestral flutists, the flute soloist is now a standard on the international touring scene. Today no one is astounded if a flutist flies in from Paris to perform for twenty-five minutes.

London is an easy one-hour commute from Paris, where I live. When you push the clock back, it actually takes no time at all to get there. You lose the time-zone advantage, unfortunately, when you fly home, which is something I have learned to accept in my constant battle against jet lag. Since I play perhaps a hundred and twenty concerts a year throughout the world, visiting four continents and about seventy different cities, it is a battle I just can't win.

In the beginning, of course, my travels didn't include engagements with major symphony orchestras. During my first "international tour" in 1953, I found myself island-hopping throughout Indonesia, performing in towns whose names I could hardly pronounce for a handful of Dutch expatriates. With time, the audience and the locales have grown in size and stature, and though I never managed to master Indonesian, my own version of English and a smattering of German and Italian have allowed me to make myself understood throughout the non-French–speaking world. One must first master the menu vocabulary; once that is out of the way, at least you can stumble along with the rest on a full stomach.

I only started adding concerts with major orchestras—or rather I began to receive and accept invitations to play with them—during the sixties. I find that orchestra rehearsals, for the most part, run smoothly. There is little more for the soloist to do than to greet the conductor and exchange a few words about the notes on which the cadenzas will end. We are professionals, well versed in the routine of touring, as indeed are the orchestras that welcome us. An orchestra will engage a different soloist perhaps as often as once a week during a season; they will rehearse their own part of any cello, piano, violin or flute concerto. There is generally one rehearsal together, and soloists expect to find the orchestra in command of its music, just as the orchestra expects to hear a soloist who knows what he is doing.

When I first started to play concerti with orchestras, the conductors were cautious and the first flute players would ignore me; they thought I was stepping on their toes, because an orchestra might schedule only a single major flute piece in any given season, a piece that the first-chair flutist used to guard protectively. Though a concertmaster or first cellist would never have behaved that way to an Isaac Stern or a Slava Rostropovich, I was breaking new ground and the flutists were both jealous and afraid. There has been a tense moment or two, but today some of my best friends are orchestral flutists, who also regularly perform as soloists with orchestras.

In the autumn of 1987, I performed the G-major Mozart Concerto in the London Festival Hall, with Sir Charles Groves conducting the Royal Philharmonic Orchestra. My reception at the Royal Philharmonic is always affectionate. I had never played with Sir Charles before, though I knew of his reputation as a distinguished and delightful conductor. A good conductor is not a rarity—most of the great orchestras have great conductors—but I don't think it's an exaggeration when I say that for every good one, you will find two bad. And among the good ones there are those who are better to work with than others, ones who are more supple and accommodating, and whose personalities are more agreeable. You can play with a fine conductor whose temperament doesn't exactly suit yours, and the concert will still be good. Some conductors, however, never manage to put you at ease.

My only hope today is that the rehearsal will not take too long. I need a good nap before an evening performance—perhaps a rather dull admission for someone who lives much of his life on a jet, but for this "jetsitter" a nap is the most important part of his concert-day routine. My body seems to know when I have a concert and becomes drowsy as the afternoon progresses. It has always been like that. Luckily on days without concerts I never feel the need to sleep in the afternoon.

Unfortunately, there has been a delay that has pushed today's rehearsal forward from 1:00 P.M. to 3:00 P.M. I flew in last night, on a regular flight to Heathrow, so I'd have time to relax. A morning flight was available on a small plane into London's new central airport, but I have had so many adventures in small planes—of which I shall say more later—that I try to avoid them whenever possible.

As usual, I stay at the Westbury Hotel off Bond Street and, with an extra two hours to kill, have a chance to go shopping, a favorite occupational therapy of mine. It always relaxes me, and only my credit cards get a workout. My main temptation is camera equipment, a yen usually satisfied in Tokyo but which I often succumb to elsewhere. Finally, having lightened my wallet and filled my stomach with a fine lunch, I am driven over to the Royal Festival Hall on the South Bank.

The place is practically empty, though there are a few people dotted around the cavernous auditorium. The concrete mass of the hall, with its greenish domed roof, created quite a stir when it opened in 1951, but today it is an accepted London landmark.

The orchestra is already onstage. In contrast to the formal attire they'll don later, the members dress casually for the rehearsal, some even in jeans; they could be perfectly ordinary people, like those one sees every day on the London buses. That is, until they pick up their instruments. These are certainly not "buskers," as they call street musicians in England.

After a few words of greeting to the concertmaster and the first flutist, I set about putting my instrument together. It is one of the two fourteen-carat-gold flutes I travel with, both of which reside in a black leather case. At home are two additional gold models—one a collector's item dating from 1869, made by the French luthier Louis Lot. I played it for the first eleven years of my career, but it is now kept locked up in a safe in Paris. For the past thirty years I have performed on the flute I've just completed assembling, which was made for me by William S. Haynes & Co. in Boston. (My two other flutes, backup instruments in case of accidents, are also from Haynes.) As the flutes are obviously quite valuable, and I'm rather fond of them, I try never to let my flute case out of sight when traveling. The one time I did, it was stolen, but that is part of another story.

It is always exciting to play in a new concert hall, or return to one that I know quite well, like the Royal Festival Hall. Nowadays there are few concert halls entirely new to me, but when I do find myself in an unfamiliar auditorium, one of the first things I do is listen carefully to the acoustics. How will my flute sound in this place? A flute may *appear* slight, but its voice can carry well even in the largest of arenas—as long as the acoustics are good.

Still, what the resonance sounds like in an empty hall can be very different from what it will be at concert time. Sometimes the instrument can seem very dry and static in rehearsal, and I worry that the concert will not sound as rich or as warm as I would like: I don't want people who come to a flute recital for the first time to be put off by a harsh, dry sonority. But when a hall is full, the sound changes dramatically. The shape and absorbency of human bodies takes the edges off a brittle timbre. That is always the case in a packed Festival Hall; there's a marvelously rich sonority that makes it a joy for a flutist to play in it.

Sir Charles Groves arrives. He is much shorter than I am, with snowy hair, and his gray trousers and comfortable blue cardigan contrast with my gray suit. But it is only proper for the guest to dress up and the host to appear at home, and Sir Charles is extraordinarily polite in the old-school English manner. We shake hands.

"Welcome, Mr. Rampal," he says. "I hope you had an easy journey?"

"Yes, yes, London is almost next door," I reply. Then, without further conversation, we proceed to the business at hand.

"What are we going to do for the cadenzas?" he asks.

In a concerto, it is up to the soloists to choose or even to write the cadenzas—that is, the unaccompanied passages in which they can display, if possible, their virtuoso technique. The cadenza first came into vogue in the second half of the eighteenth century, when it appeared in the adagio movements of concerti. Cadenzas were originally improvisations on the main theme of the movement, but they gradually started showing up in the faster sections and began to be written down. Mozart elevated this practice to new heights, writing elaborate cadenzas for his concerti, often several different ones for the same piece, depending on the talent of the instrumentalist. He was a master improviser himself, but he would write less exotic cadenzas for his students.

The tradition of a soloist writing his own cadenzas took hold during the nineteenth century. At that time, instrumentalists considered themselves to be composers as well as musicians. Today that distinction is more clear-cut, though soloists still write their own cadenzas. I have played my own cadenzas since 1946, when I first performed the Mozart D-major Concerto with a symphony orchestra in my hometown of Marseilles. (Mozart wrote two flute concertos, one in D major and the other in G major. The D-major Concerto was more popular thirty years ago than the G major, as the orchestra part is simpler and orchestras generally were not as good as they are now. Today I tend to play the G major more often.) In the exuberance of youth, I perhaps overdid my first composing efforts and put in too many twists and turns. The cadenzas were exciting, but a little long. Since then I have tempered my act but, I hope, not the excitement.

On this trip to London, I do not have the written versions of my cadenzas with me. "In the first movement, Sir Charles, I shall end on a trill that begins like this." I give a brief demonstration. If you end on a trill, it is easy for the orchestra to pick up where they left off. Classical cadenzas normally end on a trill, and some conductors have only to hear a measure or two and they know right away what to do.

"I see," responds Sir Charles. He raises his baton. After the final few bars of the first-movement cadenza, the orchestra comes in perfectly. We only need to practice it once.

Some conductors never master the art of bringing in the orchestra. A flutist can continue trilling away until his breath runs out, and the conductor still hasn't managed to rally his troops. If there isn't a trill and the cadenza ends on a specific note, there can be, shall we say, an embarrassing pause.

This actually occurs more than one would imagine. It is possible to be a bad conductor and still make a career. The world of conducting is as rife with politics as any large corporation. Those who know how to play the system can get ahead, with or without talent. When I was playing in the Paris Opera orchestra, we musicians suffered under the baton of many an execrable conductor and often wondered how they were ever allowed to take the podium. A soloist can't be a bad instrumentalist and survive the rigors of performing, but a conductor can often get away with carpet-beating in approximate time to the music. And when conductors are faced with musicians who really need their help—a young orchestra, for example—they do not have the talent to hold things together.

I love to conduct, but have the luxury of being able to do it for pleasure. However, it doesn't necessarily follow that because you succeed as a musician, you will make a good conductor. I could conduct like an imbecile, I suppose, but I do know one thing: I only conduct music that I know I *can* conduct. I know my limits, and am too busy as a flutist to study the vast orchestral repertory or be named permanent conductor of an orchestra. Few people can sustain both a solo and a conducting career. (Rostropovich and Daniel Barenboim are exceptions. When Slava was named musical director of the National Orchestra in Washington, D.C., he did not abandon the cello, nor has Danny forsaken the piano.) You have to be extraordinarily talented and you have to work very hard, harder than most mortals and definitely harder than I.

Sir Charles Groves is a conductor's conductor, the type I hope to have the pleasure of playing with again. Professional and thoroughly knowledgeable, he brought in the orchestra at the end of the first-movement cadenza perfectly, even without my written part, and he has the same classical approach to the music as I do. But as we continue through the second movement, I motion Sir Charles to stop. I feel that we are taking several important bars of the theme too fast.

"Perhaps it would be more musical like this," I suggest, and hum the line with a hair's-breath difference in the weight of a few notes.

"Yes, yes, I see. We might be able to take that a bit slower," says Sir Charles. We practice it again twice. By lengthening a beat here and there you can change the whole flavor of a piece, and it is particularly important to be sensitive to the warmth and musicality of Mozart.

It is unusual that a suggestion by a soloist to change tempi or accent will create tension with the orchestra. Unless a musician has a completely different approach to the music, there is plenty of ground for consensus. In any event it is not in my nature to storm out of rehearsals, or to make a fuss. Sometimes pieces may not sound as you would interpret them, but you are only there for one evening so what is the point of creating a nasty scene? Today, happily, the Royal Philharmonic and I are both on the same wavelength.

We proceed to the third movement. I finger through my cadenzas without playing at full power. My naptime is quickly diminishing and I begin to feel anxious to get back to the hotel.

As it is, I barely have a chance to close my eyes before the time to return to Festival Hall. I always arrive at least forty-five minutes before a concert and change in my dressing room. I hate to be rushed.

I do not do anything special to prepare for a concert, but I do like to have plenty of time to change. I travel with two evening suits and rarely wear one for two concerts running. I like to have a clean suit, and, if I put on the same one every night, it would wear out quickly. My tuxedos are custom-made by my tailor in Paris, though the cummerbund may be altered from time to time depending on my particular régime (or lack thereof), but essentially they are in the same style I have worn for forty years.

If I adhere to any dressing-room tradition, it is this: someone will always knock on the door when you have your pants down. When I am touring with John Steele Ritter, my pianist partner in recitals, and we are in the middle of changing, even before we hear a knock, the two of us simultaneously say "come in"—and invariably someone opens the door!

I ask for nothing more in a dressing room than water, preferably tap water or still, bottled water. Aerated water can produce some adverse onstage effects. It is not easy to play the flute when you burp. New York City tap water is particularly good. In fact, I must admit I find American dressing rooms in general the best. When playing a recital in Chicago, I am often given Sir Georg Solti's dressing room at Orchestra Hall. There is something about it—the atmosphere, the furniture, the piano—that makes it very commodious. I also liked the old Carnegie Hall dressing rooms for their sense of history. Goodness knows how many great musicians made last-minute adjustments to crooked bow ties in those mirrors, or hunted anxiously for a precious safety pin. The new accommodations in the renovated Carnegie are, I fear, less interesting. Perhaps in another hundred years it will have built up some traditions of its own.

This evening I am not needed onstage until after the first piece. Even without as long a nap as I would have liked, I feel more rested than before. The house is full, which is always pleasing. When I first started touring there was always a certain anxiety as to whether the public would even show up. Back in the postwar era, no one gave flute recitals. But whether I played before three hundred or one thousand people, it made no difference to the way I performed. There are no small concerts. Each time, you have a public that is judging you on your work that night. If a few hundred contented people go away and tell their friends how much they enjoyed a flute recital, the next time a flutist comes to town, the hall will be full. When I first started giving recitals across America, I would call my concert producer, George Schutz, and ask how the ticket sales were going. "Oh, I suspect we will do all right," he would say, and pause. "They might have to put a few extra chairs on the stage. Will that bother you?" I knew everything would be fine.

Which is the way I feel this evening, and, indeed, before virtually all my concerts. I am glad to say I have never suffered from stage fright. If you played as many concerts as I do and were convulsed with nerves each time you performed, you would be in hospital after two weeks. If performing is such a strain, why force yourself to do it? I do know performers who are tortured before each concert, though the audience would never realize it to hear them onstage, but if it was that difficult for me to perform, I wouldn't do it. I am not a masochist. My thoughts before a concert are generally fixed on the work at hand and the reward afterward: a good performance, a warm audience, and a sumptuous dinner. Later tonight I will be joined by Ervin Veg, who is with CBS Records in London, a delightful Hungarian who has a nose for good restaurants throughout the world. His choice can be trusted.

A few moments before my entrance, I make the short walk to the door leading to the stage. There is always a sense of tense excitement before you perform: time is suspended for a second, and you feel a wave of nervous expectancy. If it is a completely new hall with a completely new public, the feeling is even more intense. How will it sound? Will they like me? Questions speed through my mind. Nowadays, after all my touring, it is rare that I find myself in virgin territory. Sometimes it might be that I return to a place after a long absence and wonder if the audience will still remember me in the same way. That happened recently in Sofia, Bulgaria. It had been more than ten years since I had played there, but as I walked onstage, I was met with warm, welcoming applause and was very moved.

The most important part of any concert is to take possession of the hall and make contact with the audience. The public must feel that you are enjoying playing for them. This does not mean broad engaging smiles during every rest. It is a projection of oneself, one that I have never been able to analyze clearly. Isaac Stern, for example, walks out onstage in such a serious, concentrated manner you would think he was about to play a requiem for a departed friend, but as soon as he puts his violin under his chin, his face immediately becomes possessed by his music, and dynamically expressive. His violin is just another limb, and the audience feels the music completely through his body. Mstislav Rostropovich, on the other hand, bounds onto the stage with such exuberant amiability that no audience is immune to his mood. I take something of a middle ground: I am less stern than Isaac and less boisterous than Slava. I am told I have a concentrated, serious look and that my walk is determined. I make contact with the conductor and always glance at the orchestra and the audience, but my aim is to engage the public, because it's from them that I get inspiration—after all, I am not playing for myself.

There is always this romantic notion that one plays for someone special, usually a woman if you are a male performer. But this is not entirely true. In the concert hall you play for everyone, but you also play for one or two people whom perhaps you don't even know. They are out there somewhere in the first, second, third or fourth row: a couple of concertgoers who seem to catch your attention and inspire your playing. It doesn't have to be a beautiful woman—though that happens sometimes—it can just as well be a man, but it always must be someone who shows a special interest in the music. Or it could even be that you see someone who appears not to be enjoying the performance, and you play to change their mind. The reward is seeing them react at the end, knowing that you have won them over.

The best people to play for, however, are those you love. I always look to see if there are friends in the audience, or to find a member of my family. If my wife, Françoise, is there, I play for her. I need approbation and human contact.

Sir Charles understands the dynamics of a flute concerto well. The balance between the orchestra and the soloist is perfect. It is an enjoyable exchange, not overbearing, just warm and exuberant. This time there are no particular friends that I can pick out in the audience, so I have fixed my playing on a young couple who are holding hands. Mozart's melodies have a romance that I can tell has touched this pair. As we come to the end of the first movement, they let go their hold of each other to applaud.

This is a pleasing reward after my cadenza, though a trifle distracting. Generally I prefer an audience to keep quiet between movements, as it helps concentration. I keep the flute to my lips between the second and third movements to discourage interruptions and to help maintain my momentum. After a final crescendo the concerto moves softly to its close. I pause to hear the reaction, because, after all, that is in part why I am there.

There is nothing more heartening than hearing an audience erupt. I have always admitted I am a ham. However, there are hams—or as we say in France, *cabotins*—and hams. There are those who like to show off what they can do and those who like to share what they do with others. A good joke teller, for example, must be a ham who enjoys sharing his story. If you take pleasure in telling a joke, then your audience knows and appreciates it all the more.

Audiences the world over have their own character. The English, as might be expected, rarely shout their praise, though tonight they applaud affectionately enough to bring me back for three curtain calls. The concerto comes midway through the evening's program, so I do not get to give an encore—which is a pity, because I love encores. I'll play ten if the audience wants me to and won't make them clap until their palms are sore before I start playing. Usually, after the third or fourth bow (which for the longest time I always pronounced as in "bow and arrow," to the great amusement of my English-speaking friends), I will play an encore.

One plays differently for an encore: it is difficult to explain, but once the concert is finished there is a greater sense of relaxation, and even if you choose to play serious music for an encore, the interpretation can be more easygoing. This is a time to have fun, the kind of fun that you have playing music for friends. The expectations are different, and after spending an hour or so in the company of an audience, it too has become more like a friend.

In Japan the mood during a concert is usually even more subdued than in England, and you have to wait until the end of an entire concert to hear a single clap. In the United States, there is an enthusiastic response that you can feel throughout the program—at least most of the time. I also adore the Latin audiences in Europe, especially in Spain. But though I enjoyed playing before the Russian public, I did not enjoy my tour in Russia.

I have been to the Soviet Union twice, once with the Orchestre National de France as a soloist and once, twenty years ago, on a recital tour. For the recital tour, the Soviet authorities provided me with a pianist who was so bad we could hardly play the Prokofiev Sonata, a piece I had chosen specially as a tribute to the Soviets. The pianist might have been capable of accompanying a ballet practice class, which I think was her usual job, but she could not manage my programs. To add insult to injury, I had been booked into small concert halls even though large ones were available, so many people could not get tickets. I was so angered by the fiasco that I swore never to go back, though the public was forebearing and wonderfully kind. I would play for the Russian people again only if the concert management experienced its own kind of *perestroika*.

Now, at the end of the Mozart concerto, the Royal Festival Hall audience starts filing out for the intermission. I take my leave of Sir Charles and the orchestra and I am free to go.

Dressing rooms fill up very quickly. Sometimes names are hard to fit to familiar faces, but post-concert joviality can make up for any embarrassing slip of the memory. There is a sense of elation after a good concert that transports the spirit; it is as if you try to catch your breath and smile at the same time.

Tonight I have no problems putting names to faces. Those I don't know are introduced and the rest are friends, including the welcome face of Ervin Veg, dining partner. As I never eat before a concert, I am always ravenous at the finish. After a polite fifteen minutes spent chatting and signing autographs, I close the door and change.

"Come in," I call out, stepping out of my trousers, and to my great surprise there is no one knocking at the door.

I need to relax after a concert and the best way is a good meal in a friendly but not-too-chic restaurant. If a place is very posh, I sometimes am not so at ease. A Michelin three-star establishment on any non-concert night offers a wonderful experience, but after a workout, I prefer a less ritzy spot. And by ten that evening Ervin and I are in just such a place. We're drinking Japanese draft beer, eating sushi and discussing future recording plans: the perfect end to an average day in my life.

I never discuss a concert after the event. People visiting my dressing room normally tell me whether or not they enjoyed the evening, but I do not go in for lengthy critical assessment. Some concerts go better than others, and I can generally tell that for myself. I like to hear people say they enjoyed themselves but I do not want to discuss the rallentando in the second movement and its reprise in the third. I live for the moment, and at that moment the concert is over. It is more exciting to look forward to the meal to come; tomorrow, I will think of the next concert. My flight back to France is set for mid-morning and I'll go on directly to Nice to play the following night. The jaunt to London has been a great success. I have combined all the elements in my life that make living so much fun: good music, good food and good company.

My father used to say: "People who can do what they love to do for a living are the luckiest people in the world." I play the flute because my father played the flute. When I started my career in Paris after World War II, nobody made an international career as a solo flutist, but it never occurred to me that it couldn't be done.

Music was my motivation and my love, the flute my form of expressing that love. The flute, itself, has never interested me from a purely mechanical point of view, though in many ways it is the most appropriate instrument for human expression. The sound comes directly from the body, from human breath, without an intermediary.

There are no reeds, no strings, no bows, no batons. Playing the flute is just a way of making thoughts audible, as natural, in a way, as talking or singing. I am not a fanatic of flute design and do not collect flutes, and flute conventions are, for me, places to meet friends rather than to study the development of flute evolution. The flute is simply something that allows me to express what I feel is in music.

From my very first concert at the age of sixteen in a small Marseilles hall to London's Royal Festival Hall and beyond, I have tried to do just one thing: make music for people. The journey has taken me round the world many times over as I fought to have the flute mentioned as a solo instrument in the same breath as the violin, piano or cello. It has been a long road, one for which I made few plans and took along only a few indispensable items: my flute, my sense of humor, my music, and my love and respect for my first teacher— my father.

Along the way I have met and made music with some of the world's most well-known musicians and some of the most delightful amateurs. I have made many friends, whom I thank for the love and kindness they have shown me over the years. Naming them all would be to fill an entire book. Some you will meet in the pages that follow, the others know who they are. I would, though, especially like to thank a few who helped me bring my memories back to life: my old friends Robert Veyron-Lacroix, Pierre Barbizet and Christian Bourde, my personal assistant Brigitte Hohmann, and my friend Bobby (Barbara) Finn.

Most important, I have had the warmth and love of my family to accompany me every step of the way. My father was the wellspring from which I drew my first inspiration, and my mother, though sometimes reluctantly, has watched me follow the path of a musician. She would rather have had a doctor in the family who was not prone to touring the world, but she is beginning to accept that her son followed his father's path.

My wife, Françoise; my daughter, Isabelle, and her husband, Guillaume; my son, Jean-Jacques, and his wife, Virginie; and my grandchildren—Caroline, Nicholas, Elodie—remind me every day how lucky I am. My home is the center of my life, and it is from there that I renew the strength to travel far and wide. Françoise never doubted that I could make the flute a solo instrument. She put her faith in me from the day we met. I cannot thank her enough for her years of support and love.

There are people whose careers are well planned, even predestined. Mine was a mixture of chance and destiny. You might say I stumbled into a musical career because of my high school history teacher; I had to repeat a year because I failed to answer one of his questions about the Meiji of Japan. If I had not been kept back, I might well have finished my studies and become a doctor before I had a chance to become a professional flutist.

My journey started in Marseilles, where the Rampals lived under the warmth of the Provençal sun. It was there that I first heard the sound of the flute.

Music,
My Love

1

"If You Had Only Worked a Little Harder . . ."

WHEN I FIRST BROUGHT my fiancée home to Marseilles to meet my parents, it was barely a year after the end of World War II. Food was still scarce, yet in our house feelings were running high: the only son was introducing his intended to the family. This was cause for celebration, for we Marseillais have tight-knit families, and even though I had chosen a young Parisian, everyone welcomed her as if she was already a Marseillaise, as well as a Rampal. I was twenty-four and at the beginning of my musical career; if that came to nothing I would simply go ahead and begin my fourth year of medical school. Françoise, my bride-to-be, was just seventeen.

My mother had prepared a mountain of spaghetti, which commanded the center of the table. All around, everyone—my parents and my father's parents, who lived in the apartment below us—made much of Françoise and much of the meal. The spaghetti disappeared with such gusto and speed that Françoise was taken aback. She barely had a chance to say a word amid all the family's high-spirited carryings-on, and she ate what my grandmother said was hardly enough to feed a bird. To be *belle* in Marseilles means to be well-rounded physically, and my grandmother thought Françoise needed some *belle* Marseillaise padding. For Françoise, all the commotion and noise was part of an exotic world that she knew only through my descriptions, and which in reality was, for her, much larger than life.

That world is Marseilles, and its character is Provençal. It is so much part of who I am and how I live my life that I find it hard to define: it is a mixture of sun and sea, quick tempers and warm embraces. It is a place where life is lived loudly and out in the open. People talk fortissimo in the distinctive accent of the Midi—and generally all at the same time. They answer their own questions and ask others before anyone has time to breathe, and, in true South of France fashion, friends and lovers can hurl insults at one another and forget them just as quickly.

If anyone has captured this world in words and images it is Marcel Pagnol, one of France's greatest writers. Sometimes we see ourselves as imitations of the famous characters from his plays and films—César, Marius and Fanny. My parents fit the mold of the bickering, bantering Provençal couples as closely as any of our neighbors on rue Brochier in the heart of Marseilles. And though my father might, and often did, call my mother "a little fool," he cherished her as dearly as his own life. Françoise did not understand the heart of this fiction become fact, and after that boisterous meal, she took me aside.

"How can your parents possibly stay married?" she asked in alarm. "They say such awful things to each other."

To her, their particular form of conversation—a mixture of hurled slurs and loud recriminations—was evidence of impending catastrophe. I couldn't understand her alarm. I grew up with the sound of their raised voices. People say what they think as they think it, and they say it loudly. Nothing had appeared out of the ordinary to me, and I was sure that my parents' marriage was far from over.

"This is how it always is," I replied. "We are just typical Marseillais."

*

In 1919 Joseph Rampal decided to come back to Marseilles from Paris. He had finished his flute studies, won the first prize from the prestigious Paris Conservatory, and was now hoping to start a career. He had the talent to be successful in Paris, but he was destined to return home. World War I had taken one son from his parents, and he knew that ambition would not claim the other.

Joseph, the son of Lazare Rampal, a Marseilles jeweler, had started at the Paris Conservatory a year before the war. He had gone north, like his older brother Jean-Baptiste—a student of Auguste Renoir at the Ecole des Beaux Arts—to seek his fortune in the artistic center of France. The Rampals were convinced that their eldest son had the talent to be one of the world's great artists. Their younger son, they believed, might make a career in one of the great orchestras of the world.

In 1914 both brothers joined the army. Jean-Baptiste fell on the Marne front at the beginning of the war. He had left his family only weeks before and had not even had time to send them a postcard. The confirmation of his death came only after the Armistice. Through four long years there had been a lingering hope, but eventually his identification tags were found on a field with thousands of others. A white cross, in a sea of white crosses, marks the place where he is buried.

Joseph, though wounded twice in 1916, survived. After the fighting ended, he continued his flute studies and the next year won first prize for flute in a competition judged by France's most celebrated musicians, including a young Marcel Moyse, who was on his first jury. Moyse was to become the most renowned flutist of his generation and a role model for all aspiring flute students.

Moyse always told me, when I met him later in life, that he considered my father one of the best musicians of his era and that had he stayed in Paris, he would have made a distinguished career.

But for a Marseillais, family can be more important than ambition. My father's parents, devastated by the death of their eldest son, could not bear to lose their remaining child to a world centered four hundred miles away. Joseph returned to help them tend their wounds, but also to be in the town he knew, near the sea he adored and with the people he loved. He joined the Marseilles radio orchestra and taught at the Marseilles Conservatory, living with his parents in the first-floor apartment of a five-story house that the family owned. Like all the houses on their narrow street, it had a big back garden, resplendent with a large and fruitful fig tree.

My mother likes to say that she met my father "in the course of daily life." Andrée was an eighteen-year-old, finishing up school in that time of hope after the black years of war. Families that had been split and decimated were trying to get back together and resume their old ways. The voices of Marseilles were once more filling the streets, and the young people were out strolling again after dinner, watching one another and waiting for the right moment to speak. How Joseph first addressed Andrée has long been forgotten, but they gradually found themselves more and more in each other's company.

The world was, indeed, getting back to normal. Not long after that, "in the course of daily life," Joseph married Andrée and she left school. His parents moved into the apartment below, and at the end of the second year of their marriage, they started arranging their new home for the arrival of their first, and, as it turned out, only child.

I was born January 7, 1922, at 20 rue Brochier. I have few clear memories of my early years, though I am told that I was spoilt by my grandparents. The flow of life drifted between home and school, vacation and homework. I seemed to be most interested in mechanical things, such as the phonograph that held pride of place in our living room, and I could always be found in front of the radio, conducting away. Or, if I wasn't being enthralled by music, I would be building things. I remember my grandparents gave me a chemistry set and I spent hours heating up water on a small burner in some kind of experiment involving steam. The steam from the water would make a wheel turn, and I was fascinated.

Most of our vacations were spent in the center of France with my mother's sister, Susanne, her husband, René Bec, and my cousins Jacques and Christine.

We also took trips to the small coastal villa just outside Marseilles where my father kept a boat and his fishing tackle. Like most Marseillais, he was addicted to the sea and fishing. I have never shared his enthusiasm, but I loved to go with him everywhere he went. For me, my father was my hero, the strongest influence in my life.

The fact that I studied music, however, was not an automatic result of having a musician for a father. If my family had pushed for that, no doubt I would have started playing the flute when I was five, but at that time I was more interested in my pet tortoises and the small sparrows that fell into the garden from nests in the eaves of the house. The tortoises were a present my father brought back from Morocco. I would build houses and playpens for them, and feed them conscientiously. Come winter, I would watch avidly to see if I could find the place where they had decided to hibernate. Invariably I had to wait until the spring for them to reappear and never did catch them in the act of waking up.

The baby sparrows were also a springtime diversion. They would tumble into the garden on their first flights. My job was self-appointed guardian. I would sweep up the stunned birds before the neighborhood cats could make meals of them, feed them milk and sugar and give them a few "flying lessons" to keep them out of harm's way. In those days I detested cats, for it seemed to me that all they did was destroy other animals. The older I grew, the more I understood about animal and human nature. Cats will be cats, and cats will eat birds. But the law of the rue Brochier jungle, at that epoch, filled me with hatred for felines.

In my early youth, I was a promising student who regularly finished at the top of the class. My mother's dream from the very beginning was for a doctor in the family, and it looked as if I would be able to fulfill her wish. I was interested in science, in how things worked, and naturally assumed that I would do as my mother wanted. For her, the life of a doctor seemed more stable and secure than the life of a musician. Though she loved my father dearly, she preferred her son to have the kind of income and position that could be relied on from year to year; my father's patchwork quilt of positions and appointments with orchestras in Marseilles, with the radio, in the movie theater and in the resort spa of Vichy in central France during the summers, was not the kind of existence my mother wished for me. I wanted, somehow, to please them both.

The third most important person in my early years was my god-father, my mother's uncle. A godfather's traditional role is the spiritual well-being of the godchild, and Pierre Roggero, a distinguished, cul-tured bachelor, took his task seriously. For him, spirituality was not to be found wholly within the confines of the church. I was baptized a Catholic, and at that moment he pledged to watch over me, but, paradoxically, it was through his influence that I gave up going to catechism class and never took my first Holy Communion. I rarely go to Mass these days, and go into churches only to give concerts or as a tourist. I was, however, married in a church.

An anticleric by nature, my godfather provided me with a broad philosophical appreciation of the workings of the world, drawn pri-marily from secular classics. "I am not one for all the rules and regulations of organized religion," he would tell me. "It clearly has its hypocritical side. It is better to live by principles rather than regulations."

And with that he would hand me a tract or two of Voltaire. It wasn't that he didn't believe in God (many of his personal papers, found after his death, proved that he did). He just could not abide the inconsistencies he witnessed in the church. Like Voltaire, who so cleverly mocked the way Christianity was practiced by the church, my godfather used to wonder at how priests could so blithely turn their backs on the suffering of non-Catholics. He preferred to let his personal actions show what he believed.

Undoubtedly because of my godfather, I became somewhat Voltairean of spirit. As I mentioned, I am not a churchgoer, but I believe in a force stronger than man, which I suppose can be called God. I am moved by the beauty of the earth, and it is that which makes me believe in a higher power. But a formal religion? Not me.

The work of Voltaire also influenced my approach to schoolwork. I eschewed writing in the more convoluted style of romantic phrase-makers, preferring to say in short sentences exactly what I thought, *à la* Voltaire. And I learned more about "Christian principles" from the example my godfather set than from reading any catechism. He was always kind, considerate and extremely generous. He would come to dinner most nights, and after the meal we would repair to my room to study my homework together. Later, he took it as his godfatherly duty to introduce me to some of his favorite authors: Molière, Racine, Corneille, Anatole France, Victor Hugo, and, of course, Voltaire.

I received from Pierre Roggero the education of what in the eighteenth century was called *"un honnête homme"*—that is to say, one with a well-rounded knowledge of literature, the arts and music, in addition to a moral grounding in right and wrong. Pierre himself was just such an eighteenth-century "honest man," who lived—and lived successfully—by those high standards in a twentieth-century world. He had started out as a chemist and went on to make an ample fortune in the oil export and import business, though he never spoke of his work or his wealth. When he died, we learned how generous he had been to those less well-off than he.

There was not a rancorous or spiteful bone in either my godfather or, for that matter, my father. Here were two outstanding examples of how to live. My name, in fact, comes from these fine examples: the Jean in memory of my father's brother, Jean-Baptiste; Pierre for my godfather; and my middle name is Louis, for my grandmother, Louise, who was also my godmother.

My godfather died when I was twelve, but, even after his death, his image and his words stayed with me. He was my spiritual guide, and I hope in my life to have done justice to his example. I only wished he had lived to hear me play the flute.

When I was about six, I came across an old wooden flute, which thrilled me no end. It was a soprano flute, the kind used to fake an instrument in theatrical productions. I could put this instrument to my lips, blow and sound just like my father—well, not exactly like him. The noise from my little wooden flute had none of the tone, sonority or grace that emanated from my father's silver flute.

"Stop that terrible screeching," said my father, putting his hands to his ears. "You can't play that instrument. It has a false sound."

"But I want to play music."

"That is not music." And he took the flute away from me. We had a furnace in our living room that was used to warm the house; he threw the pipe into the flames.

"Your time to play music will come," he said.

For my father, an imperfect pitch, a rasping sound or just bad music could never be tolerated—even if it was his son's first musical experiment. Still, it is not easy to see a favorite toy being burned up. I was terribly disappointed, but I learned an important lesson: never settle for anything less than the very best.

"You are too young to start," explained my father, who saw how unhappy I was. "If I let you play on an instrument like that, it may ruin any talent you might have. You will learn bad habits just to make bad music, and in the long run that will not help you. Be patient, Jean; your time will come."

This early failure did not alter my desire to play music. At first, though, it appeared I would take after my father's brother, Jean-Baptiste. I started to paint with a passion, the passion that as yet I could not put into music. My grandfather gave me my uncle's paint-brushes and paint box, and I spent hours trying to capture the special light and colors of Provence. I was no young Cézanne, that's for sure, but I did show enough talent to impress even my teachers: my early efforts still hang on the walls of my family's house in Marseilles. Somehow, though, I recognized that this was not my true calling. I had never known my uncle—the role model I was, I suppose, trying to follow; the role model I wanted to follow, however, was close by me every day: my father.

*

There was no doubt about which instrument I wanted to play. Some children rebel against all that their parents say and do. I was the opposite. I worshiped my father and loved to hear and watch him play the flute. He was a man who held himself very erect and, unlike me, hardly moved when he played. He had a sonority, a sound, that was very special, very much his own, very "fleshy" and full of emotion. You could not listen to him play without being intensely aware of it. I don't say this just because I'm his son; other musicians and flutists who knew him or studied with him said it too, including the great Moyse. My father was a perfectionist in all he did, and perhaps that is why he never pushed me to play a musical instrument. He was very proud, and he could not have supported having his son play badly.

In 1928, when I was six, the family started spending the summer in Vichy. At that time Vichy hosted the only summer music festival in France. It was very fashionable, chic and tremendous fun. My father played first flute in the Orchestre du Théâtre du Grand Casino, which included about a hundred and ten musicians from the major Paris orchestras, as well as regional orchestras nationwide who came to Vichy each summer to supplement their income. Performers at Vichy were well paid, and some relied on the Vichy season for their year's earnings.

The Compagnie Thermale de Vichy, which ran the casino and spa, certainly got their money's worth. Every night there would be either a ballet production and a symphony concert simultaneously, or an opera and a concert; these were held in the different theaters that made up part of the casino. In the afternoons, concerts of popular music would be held in the Kiosk, as the bandstand was called, to entertain the cure-takers during their promenades. And at least once a week there was a major symphony concert in the Théâtre itself.

For three months each summer I waltzed around France's poshest watering hole listening to and breathing in wonderful music, attending rehearsals and concerts every day. It was here that I first saw Bruno Walter conduct, and Paul Paray, too. I heard many renowned soloists, including the violinist Jacques Thibaud and pianist Alfred Cortot. My desire to play grew and grew.

Finally, when I was twelve and a half, my father relented: I could start learning to play the flute. The change came as much from practical considerations as from anything else. He was facing a crisis at the Marseilles Conservatory: the number of flute students in his class had diminished drastically, from fifteen to three. This situation was brought about by Léon Blum, the first socialist president of France, who had initiated legal paid vacations throughout the country—something theretofore unheard of. With paid leisure time to spend, many of the French were moving away from music in favor of outdoor activities. The French are not passionately tied to music like the Germans, who have as much a need for it as they do bread. I think it must have something to do with the climate, at least in the South of France, where we Latins take our outside sporting activities very seriously. In warm countries you are more likely to pick up a game of soccer in the street than settle down to play chamber music indoors. As a result, it seemed likely that my father would have to teach music theory as well as flute in order to make a decent living. It was an idea he detested.

He had to fill up his class at all costs. He bought several battered flutes and set about repairing them. He would ask everyone he met why their sons—there were virtually no female flute players at that time—didn't play the flute. "There's no need to buy an instrument," he would say to an unsuspecting parent. "I have one I can lend your boy."

My father was still one student short at the beginning of the new term. Having me join the class, if I were good enough, would make up the numbers.

I took to the flute like, well, like the son of a Marseillais flutist would take to the flute: with passion and love. For me, playing the flute was a release for all my pent-up emotions, and to my father's delight it seemed that I had the beginnings of talent.

My grandfather had ordered a silver flute for me the Christmas before—perhaps he realized where my true desire lay, though my father was reluctant to let me follow in his professional footsteps and would not let me take lessons even after the flute arrived. Nonetheless, I took it with me everywhere and had it with me in Vichy during the summer of 1934. Once I put the instrument to my lips, I never picked up my uncle's palette again. I think I even let the paint dry on the brushes.

At the end of the summer, I presented myself at the Marseilles Conservatory for an audition. All they really wanted to see was whether one could read music a little and make a few decent sounds. At that time I had no thought of taking up music as a career, and the Conservatory was a delight: I could play music and I could have my father as my teacher. The only bad part was that these first flute lessons began early, at seven in the morning, and were followed by a full day of school. A routine was rapidly established: I got up at six-thirty, was chased noisily through a quick breakfast by my mother (who says I was always late), then accompanied my father on the brisk fifteen-minute walk to the Conservatory. Our flute class lasted two hours, and then I made the two-minute hike down the hill to the Lycée Thiers, where I joined my classmates for the rest of the day.

People have said that I was lucky because my father could give me lessons at home, but this never happened in the strict sense of the word "lesson." I took my formal classes with about fifteen other students at the Conservatory. We would each play for a few minutes and then my father would explain what was good and what was bad with each student's performance. It was an early initiation into playing in front of others.

We followed the Altès Method, an ingenious course of exercises devised by Henri Altès, a well-known nineteenth-century French flutist that takes you imperceptibly through each step. For example, the first lesson begins with the G above the staff, a note that is impossible to play unless the lips are in the correct position. Once you get that right you are on your way. If you start with a note like middle C, for example, you will not necessarily learn the correct way to position your lips; middle C can be played by blowing your nose into the flute! It is the G above the staff that helps the beginner master the correct position of the mouth, the embouchure.

The Altès Method takes the form of duets. The teacher plays the second flute, thereby forcing the students to keep time and to become accustomed to playing chamber music. If you follow the lessons diligently and have a teacher who can make sure you are learning each step correctly, you will become a good, possibly even professional-standard flutist. I had just such a diligent teacher.

At home, while I was practicing for the next day's lesson, my father would play the duets with me. I picked up what he wanted to say through osmosis, I think. We were so close that all he needed to do was indicate gently where he thought I should take more care.

"*Attention*, in the key of E flat. *Attention*, you're moving your left index finger," he would call out.

He would even correct me from a distance. When I was playing in my bedroom, he could tell if I was not fingering correctly, or if I was impeding the true sound of the instrument.

"*Attention!* Jean, you're covering the embouchure too much," he'd shout, and I would repeat the exercises until there was silence from the living room. He started my lessons with the first duets written by François Devienne, a great French flutist from the latter half of the eighteenth century.

I would always try to play duets that were just a little too difficult for me, and it was this, I think, that helped teach me good technique. I kept trying to keep up with my father, trying to master as much as he could. Perhaps this is why I made such rapid progress. At the end of a year and a half I had finished the Altès Method and was already playing relatively difficult pieces, such as the second and third movements of Mozart's Concerto for Flute in G major, the set piece for the 1935 competition at the Conservatory. I won second prize.

A year later I played a concert piece called "Ballade" by a little-known French composer named Perilhou and won the first prize.

When I was young, I liked to discover new flute pieces, but I have never enjoyed practicing anything incessantly, especially exercises. I was lucky, I suppose, because I seemed to inherit certain gifts so I didn't have to work long hours learning. I have a natural embouchure—something most people have to work hard to master. A natural embouchure means that when you put the flute to your lips it is automatically in the right position, and you can produce a true sound. The G above the staff, for instance, came easily to me. Having a natural embouchure is like being able to get on a horse and have your seat in the right place without ever having to think about it. You still have to learn when and how to pull the reins, but you are always perfectly balanced from the beginning.

I also have medium-sized lips, which makes playing easier. There are exceptions to this rule. For example, Roger Bourdin, a great French flutist, managed to produce a superb sound, and he had fat lips. And Marcel Moyse had thinner-than-average lips. The quality of the sound that I produced, too, was something I never really had to learn how to do. And I never had any trouble playing staccato notes. But I worked as hard at the rest—fingering, music theory, breath control—as any other beginner.

I can't say, though, that I was a slave to my instrument. That kind of grind takes the fun out of playing. Of course when something is new it is necessary to work to master it, but to practice from morning to night is too much for me. You have to keep life and vitality in the music, and whenever you play a piece, even if it is for the hundredth time, you must play it as if you are just discovering its beauty and are filled with the joy of that discovery. It is this that gives music its emotional appeal. Perhaps if I had practiced more I would have lost that innate sense of the music, perhaps not; perhaps that's why my father, who used to tell me I did not work hard enough, never really pushed me. He sensed that my gift was natural, inherited, perhaps even fragile, and that it should be nurtured but not smothered.

When I started out, I tried to imitate exactly the way my father played. It's part of a family's musical heritage; I suppose I had his sound in my genes. As I progressed, though, I changed and developed my own style. My father never said: "Jean, you must play like this," or "You must breathe here." He would let me develop my own interpretation, as long as it was true to the instrument. He wouldn't let me breathe in the wrong places.

I don't think it is possible to compare the two of us. We had different styles but we also had different careers. My father never pursued a soloist's career, though he had a soloist's temperament. When he did play concerti, he gave them his all. His stage presence was very strong, and I think I learned this from him, too.

He did not give solo performances very often, although he played chamber music as frequently as he could. I remember once in 1946, when he was asked to play a concerto with the Marseilles orchestra, he asked the conductor if he would invite me to play instead. My father knew I was trying to make a solo career for myself and wanted to help me. He had chosen his own career, and one concerto would not change its progress, while for me, at that time, a solo engagement was a prestigious event and I know it helped me start to make a name for myself.

The recordings I made with my father were recorded toward the end of his active career. I don't think it is possible to compare our playing styles at that point, but I enjoyed making those records because they capture us together, as we were for so many years in Marseilles. From the age of thirteen to the time when I left home during World War II, my father and I would play duets almost every day. I am glad that I have recordings of some of these, even if we had to wait nearly forty years to make them.

My father and I continued to play duets until the end of his life. I have a wonderful summer home in Corsica, on a part of the island that is as near to heaven as you can get on earth. You can hear the sea from the balcony and dine while the reflection of the setting sun bathes the hills behind you. And I have a boat, which we use to putter around the remarkable craggy coastline in search of little deserted inlets where sea urchins might be hiding. From 1968, when we bought the house, my father spent his summers there. He always used to bring his flute with him and we would look out over the sea and play duets. When he was getting very old, he lost his lower teeth and had to have false ones, which made flute-playing very difficult, though he always managed to produce his special liquid, smooth, limpid sound. "Why doesn't it sound good?" he would ask querulously.

"Panou, you aren't doing badly for an eighty-year-old with false teeth," I said, calling him by the diminutive we always used in the family. The paintings of his brother would form a backdrop to our playing, and the sea would be our metronome.

"I only wish it sounded as good as it used to," he said, as he cleaned his flute and put it away. "I will have to work a bit more." Then, as he always did, he turned his attention toward me and my playing. Before he started to speak I knew what he was going to say. It was a refrain that has echoed throughout my life.

"Ah, Jean, if you had only worked a little harder, you could have been a great flutist." He meant nothing derogatory by this remark. For him, a "great flutist" was an ideal, a specter in his imagination signifying unattainable perfection.

In the summer of 1982, Panou left his flute in Paris. I knew this was a bad sign. He died in January 1983.

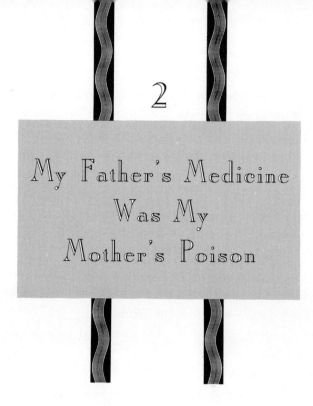

2

My Father's Medicine Was My Mother's Poison

MY FATHER'S INFLUENCE, encouragement and example have stayed with me all my life. He is with me today whenever I play and whatever I do. *You always have something more to learn, Jean, something more to correct.* My father taught me how to nurture my musical talent and also how to lead my life. Following his example has helped me maintain my equilibrium in a world that is full of potential disasters—the world of international concert touring.

My father believed that one should rely only on oneself for whatever comes to pass. You should never count on anyone, even your dearest friends, to be there to help you, even if you know they will be there most of the time. Always live life so that you have all you need within yourself. This is as true of a career as of your personal life. What you achieve will be through your own effort. It is not a question of luck—although luck always plays a part in one's life, as it has indeed played a part in mine; it is more a question of being prepared within yourself to take advantage of any luck that may come. And just as you should be ready to grab hold of a lucky chance, so should you have the capacity to cope with misfortune.

When things went wrong for my father, he could dismiss the problem without letting it eat away at him. One day we were getting ready to go fishing and we went down to the dock where we kept the boat. As we were loading the tackle, my father dropped his keys in the water. They were impossible to retrieve and annoying to replace. He didn't seem in the least concerned and continued to load the boat. I was around fourteen at the time and had invited one of my friends along with us. He could not believe that my father barely batted an eyelid.

"What would be the point?" my father said. "It would only spoil the day."

In the life of an international concert artist, many things can happen to spoil your day. If you got upset each time you missed a plane connection, lost your luggage or found no reservations had been made at the hotel, you would spend your life with your insides turned upside down and a painful ulcer. You have to be able to accommodate the disturbances of life, those events over which you have no control but which, though annoying at the time, are not fatal. I learned this lesson well from watching my father.

In 1985, I was traveling from Los Angeles to Boston when my carry-on bag containing my two golden flutes, among other things, was stolen at the L.A. airport. My partner, John Steele Ritter, had dropped my wife and me off at the TWA counter on his way to return our rental car. I checked our suitcases, and we had only our hand baggage to take care of. Françoise stayed with it as I went to reconfirm our seats. My preferred seats on airplanes are in the second row: it is a nonsmoking area, and you have a clear view of the movie screen.

I went up to the counter with my carry-on bag in my hand. I set it down for the briefest moment while I took out the tickets. As I handed the tickets to the agent, I felt someone brush past my right side. When I looked down, the small case was gone.

"Françoise," I called out, "did you take my bag?"

"No, you had it with you."

I immediately raised the alarm, and none too discreetly.

"Someone has stolen my bag! Someone has stolen my bag!" I yelled loudly.

Within moments the airport security guards appeared and I told them what had happened. At that point someone came up to me and said he had seen a young man pass the check-in line and pick up my case. The person watching had assumed the bag belonged to him.

I had a few minutes to catch my plane and a concert to give the next day at Symphony Hall. I could not wait for the security guards to search the entire airport. The first thing I did was call my friend Lewis Deveau, president of William S. Haynes & Co., the flutemakers in Boston that had made these flutes.

"Lew, do you have a gold flute I could borrow?" I asked.

"As a matter of fact we are just finishing one for a client. What's the matter, are all your gold flutes broken?" asked Lew.

"They've been stolen, and I need one for a recital in Boston tomorrow. Can you finish the flute in time?" That was all I wanted to know.

"Yes, yes, if we work through the night. Oh, Jean-Pierre, I am so sorry," he said.

"Not to worry," I told him. "As long as I have a flute for the concert, I'm happy. See you tonight for dinner, and thank you very much."

While I had been arranging the problem as best I could, Françoise and John had been panicking. They were devastated by the loss, the money and the heartache. We boarded the plane and I ordered the best champagne and proceeded to relax. We had second-row seats, I hadn't seen the movie before (a small miracle with the amount of flying I do) and was being looked after by a charming flight attendant. My reaction was not heartless, just expedient. Why spoil good champagne and six hours of peace in a comfortable chair?

We landed at Logan Airport and by chance ran into my friend Michel Debost, the wonderful French flutist, who had already heard of my misfortune from Lew Deveau.

"I'm so sorry about what happened to your flutes," said Michel.

"*Tant pis!*" I replied. "Yes, it's annoying, no, I'm not pleased, but we have reservations for a lobster dinner at Anthony's Pier 4, and right now I'm looking forward to that. Come with us."

Michel joined the party and we had, as I thought we would, a splendid evening, consuming wonderful fresh Maine lobsters in vast quantities. Françoise was still worrying about the flutes when she turned out the light in our hotel room. I was already asleep. I knew I would have a gold flute for the concert, and that was all I needed to know.

In the middle of the night the phone rang. Bobby Finn, a close friend and former student who now works for CBS Records, told me that Nancy Northworthy from my manager's Los Angeles office was trying to contact me. The police at the L.A. airport had found her name and number wrapped inside one of the towels in the bag— a phone message that Françoise had obviously scooped up when she packed. The police wanted her to come to the airport and identify the bag. Bobby told me to expect a call from L.A.

Half an hour later the L.A. police called and asked me to describe the contents of the bag.

"There's an electric razor, an address book, music scores and a black leather case with the initials JPR engraved on it in gold," I said, holding my breath.

"Inside the leather case we have what look like six bits of broken pipes. In gold. Would you know anything about these?" asked the policeman.

"Yes, I know a bit about them," I replied, almost laughing.

I proceeded to describe the flutes and give their identification numbers. I, of course, was delighted. Nancy agreed to be my courier and fly across the country with the flutes. I went back to sleep immediately. I used Lewis Deveau's new flute for the Symphony Hall concert and persuaded him to sell it to me and make a new one for his other client. My father would have been proud of me.

*

My mother would have preferred that my black leather bag contain a stethoscope and a thermometer and not six gold pipes! She has always been—and even today, at the age of eighty-six, is still—against music as a career. The uncertain income, the necessity of touring, the fickleness of the public: these are the things she fought about with my father. One musician in the family was already too much for her.

When I was a teenager she was always concerned that I do better at the Lycée than at the Conservatory. And, to her delight, I routinely came in at the top of the class—at least until that fateful day when my father needed another flute student. The flute put an end to my spree of academic achievement, and from then on even my extracurricular activities involved music. I chose friends like Christian Bourde and Pierre Barbizet, who were similarly obsessed. Like me, each played an instrument—Christian, the violin, Pierre, the piano—and like me they loved to scour Marseilles's music shops for scores. We made quite a trio; the three musicateers, you might say: Pierre, short and swarthy; Christian, of medium height and thin, with sandy colored hair; and me, tall and a bit on the skinny side (then). We put a great deal of force into life and music. We would be in and out of one another's homes trying out this piece or that, sometimes classical, sometimes jazz, sometimes contemporary, sometimes Baroque. We also bought all the early Hot Jazz Club recordings and wondered at the new sound of a young violinist called Stéphane Grappelli and guitarist Django Reinhardt. It was our age of discovery, and though we put most of our energy into those things that all teenage boys dream about, we also found plenty of time to play music together.

In fact, C. Bourde, P. Barbizet and J.-P. Rampal made a recording of these early experiments. It was a gift for Christian's father on his birthday, made at one of those make-your-own-record places in Marseilles. I think we played a trio by Loeillet and Pierre played a

Schumann piano piece. I don't consider that ancient record part of my discography, but Mr. Bourde was delighted and we had great fun in the process!

When we musicateers weren't playing our instruments, we were probably at the cinema. This was the great era of the American musical, and Fred Astaire was my idol. When I first went to Hollywood, my teenage awe propelled me to try to get in touch with Astaire. I succeeded in calling him once, but we never met. In Marseilles in the thirties, his aura of elegance and romance moved my friends and me, as it did millions of others, to believe in a world where heroes could sweep heroines off their feet with a song and a dance. There was a movie theater in Marseilles that showed all the English-language films in their original versions, and we could be found there most weekends, marveling at what our suave idols were up to, noting how they dressed and later trying as best we could to copy their style.

I was quite a dandy at that time, and took great pains with my appearance. After all, I had turned sixteen and was beginning to show more than a passing interest in the members of the opposite sex. I spent half my pocket money on music scores and the rest on clothes. I would rarely wear the same suit two days running, and I would practice my own versions of Fred Astaire dances. I never went so far as to learn tap dancing, but I did master a swooning waltz, or at least I thought I did, and a few neat turns that I hoped would get the proper attention. We were probably as graceful as young elephants, but I can't remember stepping on too many toes.

Each Sunday there would be what we called a "surprise" party at the house of one of our friends. The girls would bring the food and the boys would provide the wine. We would dance to the new jazz records of Duke Ellington, Count Basie, Fats Waller and others, showing off our best. The problem was finding a Ginger Rogers to share the limelight.

Dancing was about as close as we got to the girls of our own age. In those days there was no fooling around before marriage, and we boys all lived in fear that if we went too far, too quickly, we would be forced to end our studies and marry the young lady in question. Our natural desires had to be satisfied elsewhere, and luckily one could find the means. Married ladies were fair game, in a manner of speaking, and Marseilles, being the bustling port that it was, had its share of brothels.

These institutions were grand affairs, similar to the famous 122 Club in Paris. 122 rue de Provence was a rendezvous for the international aristocracy. It was sumptuously decorated and boasted a fine restaurant—so fine, in fact, that men would often take their wives to dine there on nights when they were not availing themselves of the other services 122 rue de Provence provided. The plush Marseilles brothels were of this luxurious kind, and their ladies of the night were no ordinary streetwalkers; they were beautiful artists. Any proper young man from a good Marseilles family who did not want to marry at an early age could gain experience and find his entertainment there. One might have started out as a baby elephant here too, but with a little instruction one also managed to avoid stepping on too many toes.

*

My musical influences at that time were also vast and varied. I absorbed everything I could from my father: his style of playing, his likes and dislikes. Whether a piece was by Mozart or an unknown composer, he enjoyed any music that *sang*. If the music touched an emotional chord, he loved it.

I feel the same way. There is good music and there is great music, and you can like a piece by Bach better than a piece by an inferior composer, but at the time you play *any* piece you must love it with all your heart in order to play it well. I always say it is like making love to a woman. You have to love the woman you are with, or else you cannot make love at all. Music is such an act of love. With my friends and teachers I used this passion to explore the musical landscape.

One of our favorite pastimes was attending an optional two-hour class given each week by Jean Prat, our professor of letters at the

Lycée Thiers. Prat was a good amateur pianist who could sight-read almost anything, as well as a learned musicologist. He was short, with a distinguished air, and though naturally shy, he became animated when he spoke of music, gesticulating broadly. Prat helped us learn the language we needed to discover and discuss what we liked and disliked about music. I had a passion for the Romantics, in particular Weber, though I never particularly liked Chopin or Liszt (I have since changed my mind!). Prat championed Mozart and Bach, my friend Pierre Barbizet adored Beethoven. Our discussions enlivened the class of twenty or so music lovers, and the two hours would sometimes turn into whole evenings, with Pierre and me helping Professor Prat demonstrate musical examples. I stayed close to Prat through the years and was always delighted to see him at each concert I played in Marseilles. He added fuel to my musical fire and helped me appreciate the more scholarly aspects of music.

My friends were my other great musical influences, and their interests spanned the centuries. Pierre Barbizet already knew that he wanted to become a professional musician, and he discussed and played all music with a fervor that impressed and inspired me. Together we played most of the major symphonies and violin concerti by Beethoven and Mozart, transcribing them on the spot for flute and piano. In fact, we played anything we could get our hands on.

It was from another friend from Marseilles, Herman Moyens, that I acquired an interest in contemporary French music. Herman was an enthusiastic pianist who, although he sometimes lacked the technique to play the more difficult pieces, could always give you the sense of the music, primarily because of his tremendous *addresse*— that is to say, the gusto with which he played. He was two years older than I, and ended up in Paris ahead of me. Once there, he soon became involved with a music radio station, the Club d'Essai, and during the war, it was Herman who first helped me make radio recordings. He also introduced me to composers such as André Jolivet, whose pieces I premiered around the world.

My interest in the eighteenth century was fueled by Christian Bourde's elder brother, André, an excellent pianist who adored Baroque and Rococo music. He passed on his enthusiasm to the trio of young fanatics—*mélomanes* as we were called. And my father at that time had given me as a present the right to order one piece of music a week from a music publisher friend of his in Paris. In the mid-thirties, a German company—Nagel Musik Archiv—started printing previously unpublished Baroque music, and I began to build my first library of musical scores with pieces by Telemann, Bach, Handel and also Haydn.

At that time, few people were interested in the Baroque. You might hear Bach played regularly and perhaps some Scarlatti harpsichord music, but Telemann was new. Few people had heard of Monteverdi, and even Vivaldi was not widely known. I waited impatiently each week for my new score to arrive. *This* was virgin territory I was delighted to discover.

*

I enjoyed playing in front of my classmates in Jean Prat's seminars, and I enjoyed the impromptu concerts that Barbizet and I would give. But the idea of playing professionally was a constant dream. In the end, it didn't take me long to move out of the music room and onto the stage. I started playing in the Orchestre des Concerts Classiques de Marseilles beside my father when I was still at school, probably when I was about fourteen or fifteen. One day the second flutist fell ill, and my father suggested to Paul Paray, the conductor at the time, that I fill in.

"He can play well," my father told Paray. "You won't have to worry."

Paul Paray had immense respect for my father, and took him at his word. My father, however, though confident of my ability, left nothing to chance. We were playing the second suite from Ravel's *Daphnis et Chloé*. I had never played in a professional orchestra before, and I had not had any rehearsals.

"Don't worry, Jean," said my father. "I'll be there with you."

The second flute part is difficult, but it essentially plays only in answer to the first flute, so it is rare that both flutes are playing different things at the same time. My father helped me through it, for he was able to play most of my part with me, as well as his own. It was not a startling debut and I don't think I could have made it on my own.

Maître Paray appeared pleased with the result, and within a short while I had become the regular second-chair flutist in the orchestra. I must admit that I was at first terrified of Paray. He was very stern, and had a fierce, eagle's glare that paralyzed many of the younger musicians. I remember once when my father came down with the flu and I played the first-chair flute for the first time, I was almost too scared to perform. But Paray was very professional with me. He seemed to expect that I would have no problems with the program: Beethoven's *Eroica* Symphony and a *Leonore* Overture and César Franck's *Psyche*. His confidence inspired me, and I rose to the occasion. It wasn't the greatest performance, but Paray nodded his approval at the end. I mopped my brow.

Since then, I had the honor to work with him on many occasions. His tough exterior concealed a loving spirit, and orchestras around the world adored playing under him. I remember giving a series of concerts in Israel with him when he was about ninety years old. Offstage, I must admit, he looked his age: a bent, graying nonagenarian. Once he raised the baton, however, the metamorphosis was extraordinary. He shed half a century! The Israeli Philharmonic was playing the overture to *Fidelio*, and you would have sworn a middle-aged man was conducting.

After the performance, we would dine together. Paray would change into his pajamas and take his place in the dining hall of the musicians' residence. He always ate an enormous bowl of soup with tremendous concentration.

One night his wife, Yolande, leaned over to me and in a whisper said: "Please don't give Paul any wine."

Any semblance of deafness vanished from Paray's face.

"After all I have been through, after all the work I have done!" he sputtered. "Life would not be worth living if Jean-Pierre can't even serve me a glass of wine with my dinner!"

The eagle glare that I first saw on the stage in Marseilles was once again trained on me, and I served him the wine immediately. At ninety, he had earned anything he wanted, I felt.

*

My first professional recital was with Pierre Barbizet, when we were both sixteen years old. We were progressing apace at the Marseilles Conservatory. I had won my first prize in 1937, after only two years' work, and Pierre won his, too. Though I had played well during my first year, the jury decided not to award me the first prize then— and it was for the best. "You have time," my father said. "And you have much work to do." How often had I heard that before!

Barbizet and I organized a flute and piano recital for July 16, which unfortunately was just before our baccalaureate exam. We chose to play a difficult piece by Herman Lilge, a contemporary of Hindemith, as well as the Sonata in A major by Bach, the obligatory Beethoven for Pierre and, of course, Mozart for me.

I can't say I was at all nervous. The Salle Mazenod holds about four hundred and fifty people, and it was full that night. Of course, my entire family and Pierre's turned out, but there was also a large group of the paying public. We dressed in our best dark suits (still taking care to look as much like Fred Astaire as possible).

I know we were both very relaxed. We had been playing together for several years and often gave informal recitals for our friends. The size of the hall was exciting, not terrifying. Perhaps it was here that I had the first inklings of desire to be a soloist; I liked the limelight and I liked performing. Playing before this many people, all of whom applauded loudly at the end, was just the kind of encouragement we needed.

We took our bows at the end, and launched into an encore. If I remember correctly, we played several. As I have said before, I like encores. It shows that you are appreciated and that you appreciate your audience. Pierre and I were in our element.

3

The War Years:

Marching to the Beat of a Different Drummer

IN 1939 I was a seventeen-year-old high school student starting to make a name for himself locally as a musician. I played second flute to my father in the Orchestre des Concerts Classiques de Marseilles under Paul Paray, and I performed chamber music with my friends. The rumblings of war sounded loud and troublesome. Food was becoming harder to find, and my Jewish friends from school were beginning to hear horror stories from the north. I was too young to join the massing French forces, but not too young to understand that life was about to change.

When Hitler invaded Poland, England and France declared war on Germany in September 1939. Then, after seven months of the "phoney" war, the Germans marched into France in June 1940. The shock of the capitulation came shortly after that, as the Germans outflanked the French and made for Paris. Of course, we went on living, working and studying, but France was now under German occupation, an unthinkable thought. The Germans split France into zones. They used their troops to control the strategic north and the Atlantic seaboard, and there was a so-called unoccupied zone, where the government of Marshal Pétain exercised nominal control over a square that stretched north from Nice to just below the Swiss border, west to below Tours and south to the Pyrenees.

The border between these zones cut a visual scar into the heart of France. Sometimes, if they happened to find themselves on the border, villages were arbitrarily divided and people who lived a street away from their relatives found that they needed special papers just to cross town. Although the unoccupied zone was supposedly still under French authority, and swarms of refugees headed south to escape the Germans, in reality France was controlled by the Nazis. Pétain led a puppet government in Vichy, and Paris was overrun by the Reich. At the end of 1942, the Germans did away with the idea of an unoccupied zone and their forces took over all across France.

Even in Marseilles, the major city of the so-called unoccupied region, Germans were in the streets and around the port from the summer of 1940 onward. They prohibited fishing, the main source of fresh protein for the city, and took for themselves all the food the area produced. The Midi suffered badly from lack of supplies. Unlike the north, the South of France raises citrus and grapes but has few other agricultural resources. The supplies of meat and almost all vegetable produce were cut off, and we could not even develop the kind of black market that evolved in Paris, because there were no outlying produce farms. We lived on thin soups, and more thin soups. Even I was little more than skin and bones at that time.

Music—playing and listening—was my sustaining outlet. Almost overnight Marseilles became the center of musical France. As the Germans moved into Paris, the musicians moved out. The Orchestre National de France, the Orchestre Radio Symphonique and the Orchestre Lyrique all relocated to Marseilles, bringing more than three hundred musicians into the city, as well as many renowned soloists, including harpist Lily Laskine—who was to become one of my dearest friends—pianist Jeanne-Marie Darré and the Quatuor Pascal. The town resonated with music a young performer could not ignore; such artists saw me through the terrible depression of the Occupation, and later, when I re-encountered some of these new friends in Paris, they were very helpful to my career.

There were continuous symphony and chamber music concerts. Each Sunday, the Dominican church actually incorporated a concert into the Mass. And the Comtesse Pastré, or "Lily" as everyone called her, a noted Marseillaise and a member of one of France's oldest philanthropic families, took advantage of all this talent and hosted evenings of dance, music and theatrical performances in the grounds of the rundown Château Montrédon or in her own house nearby. My father was a frequent guest there, and I often had the pleasure of playing for the comtesse, too.

Lily Pastré was an extraordinary woman who, like many in that dangerous time, came to the aid of those worse off than she. She not only encouraged and supported an artistic circle; she also helped hide and protect many Jewish artists and refugees. One such was Jan Meyerowitz, a Jew who came to her by way of Italy, bringing with him a certain flair for music; he was in part responsible for my indoctrination to opera.

I was twenty years old at the time, and open to all kinds of new musical ideas. Meyerowitz was a fine pianist, who could sit down and play the whole of Mozart's *Don Giovanni* or the complete works of Offenbach and Verdi. This was something new to me, and I was a willing listener. The nineteenth-century grand operas still seemed gaudy and melodramatic, but I loved the pared-down piano versions Meyerowitz served up. If anyone had told me then that I would one day play in an opera orchestra, I would have considered them out of their minds, but music of any sort was always intriguing, and opera *à la* Meyerowitz was something fascinating.

I had heard opera before, at the Marseilles Opera House, because my grandfather Lazare Rampal was an enthusiastic opera buff; he was slightly deaf and had a front-row subscription to compensate for his poor hearing. From an early age I understood the connection between the human voice and the instrument, and even if I didn't particularly enjoy the stage spectacles, I could appreciate the sounds. My favorite tenor was Georges Thill, one of the great voices of his time. I heard him sing Lohengrin in Marseilles when I was barely out of my teens. He had a way of singing, of phrasing, that immediately touched me; his melodic line was as instrumental as it was vocal. I realized then that great singers must "play" their voices as if they were instruments, and that great musicians must be able to play their instruments as naturally as they speak. I think this helped me to have natural, easy phrasing and natural breathing on the flute. Thill mastered this with his voice in the same way that Pavarotti and Domingo do today. In my playing I have always tried to "tell" my music as I might tell a story to a friend.

*

As a member of the Orchestre des Concerts Classiques and as the son of the best flutist in town, I was immediately accepted into the milieu of emigré Parisian artists. I went to concerts when I could and also played in many alongside the newcomers. I knew the musical director of the Dominican church, who used to organize what were called "artist masses" and often included me in the program.

I first met and played with harpist Lily Laskine in that Dominican church. I was just a youngster and she was already much more than a well-known star, though her generosity to an unknown musician was wonderful. She would often come to my house to have dinner with my family. One night the radio was broadcasting a Puccini opera, and I threw up my hands in horror.

"This is such overblown, vulgar music! Give me Bach and Mozart any day." Even Meyerowitz hadn't convinced me that Puccini knew what he was doing. But Lily, who was a small, exquisite lady then in her fifties, sighed.

"You will see, Jean-Pierre. Later, when you are older, you'll see what is good in Puccini. Later, when you've had more romantic experiences, you'll hear Puccini again and you'll understand him."

She was right, of course.

For our first concert together in the Dominican church, Lily and

I played the second movement of Mozart's Concerto for Flute and Harp. We played that particular movement for two reasons: first, it requires fewer strings and there are no oboes or horns as in the other movements; and second, space in the church was limited. Also, the second movement is an andante, slow and suitably respectful for a church setting. At that time, to play an allegro con brio in a house of God was regarded as profane. So was applauding. It was only after the war that Lily and I started hearing the warm response of an audience, sometimes even in a church. Lily and I played and recorded together for more than thirty-five years, until she was too fragile to manage her magnificent harp. She died in 1988.

*

The musical merry-go-round in Marseilles came to an abrupt halt in 1943. For the first three years of the war, I continued my studies and music, but upon turning twenty-one I had to present myself to the authorities. There was no army into which one could be drafted, but the youth of occupied France needed to be kept busy in ways the Nazis felt were not threatening. France had mobilized hundreds of thousands of young men at the outbreak of war, and now something had to be done with this assembled force. A mere hundred thousand were kept in uniform for "peace-keeping" duties in the unoccupied zone, but this still left legions of young men of fighting age suddenly without a cause.

I was fervently anti-Nazi, but I was neither an active member of the Resistance nor a Pétainist, and neither were my friends. During the early part of the war, few Frenchmen joined the Resistance, and most of those first heroes came from the Communist party. Our own resistance was with a small "r." We just wanted to have as little to do with the Germans as possible.

One day there was a knock at the door. My father went to answer it. Through the open doorway I could see a young German soldier.

"Are we under investigation?" my father asked.

"No, Mr. Rampal," said the young officer. "This is not an official call. Am I right in thinking that you teach the flute?"

"Yes," replied my father, still somewhat suspicious.

"I am an amateur flutist, and I wondered if it might be possible for you to give me some lessons while I am here in Marseilles?" asked the German, very politely.

At first my father hesitated, then he answered, "I'm sorry, but I cannot. You have to understand the position I find myself in. You are a German officer in my hometown of Marseilles—that is to say, you are the conquerors and we are the conquered. I don't know how I can give lessons to you under these circumstances, unless I am ordered to do so. I had a brother killed in the last war. It would be too difficult for me. Personally I have nothing against you, but I cannot give you lessons. I hope you understand."

"I do," said the young man, and left.

My father came back into the living room, where my mother and I were waiting.

"Perhaps I did the wrong thing," he worried. "Perhaps there will be reprisals. But I could not give him lessons."

The young man must indeed have understood, because we heard nothing more, either from him or from any other Nazi officials, except when they sent out notices rounding up young men for work camps. Now my main concern was to avoid being sent to Germany.

In August 1940, Général de la Porte du Theil, who reported to Marshal Pétain in the unoccupied zone, was given the go-ahead to organize the Chantiers de Jeunesse. This was a a kind of Boy Scout army-without-arms that stressed moral and physical hygiene; the general hoped it would be a way to mollify the youth of France, as well as keep them busy. All young men of an age for military service were called upon to spend nine months in one of the various Chantiers that then dotted unoccupied France. You either joined a Chantier or you were shipped to Germany with a work party.

To me, the idea of going to Germany was unthinkable; the Chantiers de Jeunesse was the only alternative. To soften the blow, my friend Christian and I joined up together. We had both just started medical school, but neither of us was far enough along in our studies to be considered useful in any hospital unit, so we were accepted as ordinary recruits.

The first shock was separation. Because of the alphabetical difference between our family names, we weren't sent to the same camp. I went to Nyons, about eighty miles north of Marseilles, and he was in Die, another twenty or so miles farther away. There, we woke up to the realities of forced labor. As mere recruits we had to spend our days doing exhausting physical work—tree-felling and ground-clearing—on very little food. The harshness of the life and the futility of the work jarred my existence. We cadets were doing nothing to help the future of France, and nothing to help ourselves.

My escape, again, came through music. I applied, along with about five hundred other hopefuls, for a place in the Orchestre de Chantiers de Jeunesse, which was located at Châtelguyon, not far from the occupied zone in central France. As most of the would-be symphonists were rank amateurs, I had little trouble securing the position of first flutist.

Châtelguyon had been a luxurious spa that shared the thermal resources and some of the prestige of nearby Vichy. Even though the arrival of the quasimilitary Chantiers de Jeunesse, which made its headquarters there, had changed the face of the elegant resort, it was a far cry from the labor-camp existence in Nyons.

There to meet me on arrival was a veritable soul mate: an educated musician who had a lust for chamber music and a sense of humor droll enough to take the boredom out of many a day in camp. Jean-Louis Audirac played the flute, and we shared the same disrespect for the Boy Scout brigade in which we found ourselves. Two flutists, if they put their minds to it, can disrupt or distort pretty much any piece of music, and I must admit that Audirac and I, with an accent here and a whistle there, tried the patience of our worthy, but not very musical, conductor, Commissaire Pardoël. His ear, as we quite quickly found out, could not locate the source of those odd sounds in the orchestra.

Audirac was the leader of my troupe and an ally for my next

challenge: to find a way for Christian to join me. Poor Christian was still cutting down trees in the backwoods of Die. His hands were torn to shreds and he hadn't practiced the violin for weeks, but he was willing to make the trek to Châtelguyon for an audition. He played the first movement of Mozart's Fifth Violin Concerto for Commisaire Pardoël (excruciatingly badly). Pardoël, though a poor musician, could not help but recognize Christian's deficiencies—even my deaf grandfather would have heard something was wrong. Nevertheless, Jean-Louis and I were able to persuade Pardoël that Christian was much better than he played and that he was the kind of recruit—well-educated and well-spoken—who would do the orchestra good.

Overnight, life became eminently more livable. I had music and my best friend, and, even if we did have to get up at the crack of dawn, wear khaki uniforms and play military marching music, it certainly beat work camps in Germany and forced labor in France.

When Christian arrived at Châtelguyon, there was no room for him in the ordinary barracks. He was assigned to a small shack that doubled as the instrument repair workshop, which he shared with the designated instrument doctor. As I saw that the two lived better in their relative privacy, I moved over from my crowded dormitory to join them. We managed to make quite a life for ourselves under the austere circumstances.

Though we were supposed to spend the day building up our physical morale, Christian and I used to slip back to bed after the morning reveille. We ignored many of the regulations, which didn't appear to bother our superiors—probably because they, too, realized the futility of the whole operation. We did make sure we were on time for rehearsals and concerts. I was something of a star in the orchestra—a one-eyed man in the kingdom of the blind, with my tinny regulation flute—and Commissaire Pardoël respected my ability.

Our afternoons in the instrument workshop were often spent playing chamber music. Pardoël, for all his lack of musical talent, managed to secure many scores, and he passed these on to his enthusiastic flute soloist. I hunted out the best musicians in our motley crew, and we would converge in the workshop to amuse ourselves.

We had tea at four in the afternoon and then played all the interesting music we could find to fill up the tedium of our exile.

Our concert schedule, by comparison, was far from riveting. For six months we played a more or less identical program, both at Châtelguyon and on the small tours we made: Schubert's Symphony No. 8 (the *Unfinished*), Rossini's *William Tell* Overture, a popular song or two and maybe Beethoven's *Egmont* Overture. I was sometimes given the chance to play a Mozart flute concerto, but the orchestral accompaniment left much to be desired.

Pardoël, who had been the head of music for the 94th Infantry— a post about the equivalent of a high school marching band conductor—had dreams of a classical conducting career. His enthusiasm, however, was coupled with a marked lack of talent, which made our forays into serious music disastrous. He conducted Schubert's *Unfinished* Symphony for six months—always with the score in front of him and always as if he were discovering the music for the first time: he appeared constantly surprised and never entirely at one with the orchestra. He marked the beats with all the vigor and mentality of a carpet cleaner. To this day, I can hardly hear that beautiful piece without flinching. When you play something day after day, and you play it badly, you destroy it, no matter how great a work it is. Schubert did not survive Pardoël. Fortunately, I did.

*

There was a clarinetist in the orchestra named Giraudo, who was contemplating an "escape." He knew that Pardoël respected musicians, and he also knew that the Paris Conservatory—France's most prestigious music school—was holding its annual auditions despite the Occupation. He suggested that the two of us ask Pardoël for permission to go to the capital. I must admit that at first the idea did not inspire me; the thought of going on with a professional musical career came in a long way behind my desire to evade the stupid drudgery of the Chantiers de Jeunesse. But the idea of a trip to Paris, a city I had visited only once before—with my grandparents, for the 1937 World's Fair—was enticing. I had shown no interest in Paris in 1937, but ironically the only clear impression I retain from that trip is of a tour through the German pavilion, where there was a display of flutes made out of transparent plastic.

Pardoël was, I suspect, proud to see some of his musicians willing and able to appear at the Conservatory audition. He gave his permission, and I immediately telephoned my father.

"It's for fun," I told him. "It's not that important. I just need to get away from here for a while."

I should have known what his reaction would be.

"If you are going to try to get into the Conservatory, you must succeed. If you don't get accepted, I shall be very angry. You are a good musician, and you have our name to uphold," he said.

He was on the next train from Marseilles to Châtelguyon, a silver Louis Lot flute in hand. Although at that time the journey was long and dangerous, my father wanted me to have the best instrument possible for my audition. He could not conceive of my playing on anything less than the best flute available. For me to succeed meant more to him than to me. I played my audition pieces through for him in the shabby back-room barracks at the camp. As usual, he didn't give me a formal lesson, simply continued the advice and counseling of our happier times in Marseilles. *Attention*, don't cover the embouchure. *Attention*, do this, do that. . . . We might have been back—and I only wished we were—in our living room at 20 rue Brochier. Satisfied with my preparation, he left for the south, and I headed north to Paris with Giraudo.

There were seven or eight musicians on the Conservatory jury, and I must admit I was worried about being accepted. My experience for the most part had all been in Marseilles, a provincial town, and the idea of Paris seemed awesome. Was I really as good as I thought I was? My father's words sounded as loud in my ears as the music: "The moment you begin to play you must say to yourself, 'I am the best in the world.'"

I was chosen in the first round.

The delight of success was tempered with the knowledge that I must relinquish my place and return to the camp. I had done well by the family name, upheld its honor for my father's sake, but unfortunately could not go ahead and continue with my studies—I did not have the papers that would permit me to stay in Paris, and I wasn't sure how to get them. My pass from the Chantiers de Jeunesse had expired. Finally, I went to see Gaston Crunelle, the flute professor. "Delighted to meet you," I said. "I'm sorry I can't stay any longer."

But he had a different idea. He told me I had the right to defer entering the Conservatory for a year. "Who knows what will happen between now and then?" he said. "Who knows?"

I left Paris with my seat at the Conservatory reserved, but didn't really think I would ever be able to use it. My clarinetist friend did not succeed in getting a place, and I lost touch with him. Mr. Giraudo, wherever you are, I can never thank you enough for having thought of taking me with you to Paris.

*

When we returned to Châtelguyon, Christian greeted me with muted congratulations. News that the Class of 1942 (boys born in 1922) was being sought for the Service de Travail Obligatoire—work parties—in Germany was rapidly spreading through all the Chantiers. There would be no time to secure permission to return to the Conservatory. The Germans had been drafting young men throughout the year, starting with those born in 1920. Now my year had come up. Christmas was approaching, and we were convinced that our only gift from the occupying forces would be a ticket to Germany. We had to find a permanent way out.

Christian's father was a famous surgeon in Marseilles, head of the hospital faculty there and a powerful force in medical circles. And though we did not know it at the time, he was also a powerful force in the Marseilles Resistance. Christian had told him about our fear of being sent to Germany and our desire to escape from the Chantiers. He wrote to the head of our unit on hospital stationery, saying that we were requested to take the entrance exam for the Military Medical School in Lyons.

It did not occur to the first paper-pusher who received the request for leave to wonder why we should be sought out by a medical school we did not have the right to attend. He saw the official letterhead, noted the formally worded invitation, and stamped his approval.

"When the first stamp is there the second will be easier." And after the second stamp, I said, "We will have no more problems."

It may be the only time I have thanked God for bureaucracy. Our permits took a whole day to process, and we waited for them anxiously. Finally, with the stamp barely dry on our papers, we headed toward the depot where we had surrendered our civilian clothes when we first joined the Chantiers. It was nearing the end of the day, and the officer in charge was already closing up shop. The last thing he needed was two anxious cadets panting at his door, but with a little persuasion we managed to cajole him into handing over our wrinkled garments. Christian wanted to give in and wait until the next day, but I was adamant that we leave right away. Those "official" stamps seemed far too chancy. We had already missed one bus that would have taken us to the station at Riom, and the prospect of a long, cold walk was sapping Christian's resolve.

"We have six kilometers to go," he reminded me, as we headed toward the night train to Marseilles. "Shouldn't we just wait for the next bus?"

"We don't even know if there is one," I replied. "And even then we don't know what time the train is supposed to leave. I think we should get to the station *fast*. We should start right now."

"It might be easier to take the day train in the morning," Christian said, as we started away from Châtelguyon. But we continued to walk, and both felt that the eyes of Châtelguyon were following us.

"I have a feeling that if we wait until tomorrow we might not make it," I said. And we picked up the pace.

We walked in silence for a long way, moving to the side of the road each time headlights came up behind us. We couldn't afford to be seen nor risk hitching a ride. The drivers of those cars maybe already knew we were truants, and were playing a cat-and-mouse game.

"Do you think we'll get there?" asked Christian, as what we thought were the lights of Riom came into sight.

"Do you think the train will still be there?" I asked in return. Neither of us had any answers.

An hour later we were rolling south, slowly, toward Marseilles, on the night train. We could hardly believe it. We had had every reason to flee as we did. The very next morning our fathers were at the station to meet us, armed with telegrams from Châtelguyon demanding that we return immediately. But the mice had fled the trap, and the cat's claws did not reach quite as far as Marseilles. It was Christmas, the streets were bustling with people home for the holidays, and my father felt I would be safe hiding out with the family, at least until the New Year. Christian would do the same thing. Neither of us could envisage going back to the Chantiers, but in order to avoid imprisonment we both had to go our separate ways. Christian managed to wangle a medical exemption from the service through the help of his father; I realized that in Paris I could remain fairly anonymous and decided to claim my place in Gaston Crunelle's class immediately. It was then that I recognized how clever he had been to persuade me to defer my acceptance rather than give up the idea entirely. My father was too well known in Marseilles for me to stay hidden there for long, and I would have a better chance of escaping attention in Paris. My musical studies would be my alibi. My medical career would have to be put on hold.

4

Music
by
Default

TRAVELING THROUGH FRANCE in 1943 was, I suppose, dangerous. Traveling through France in 1943 without the correct papers was potentially insane.

For some reason, though, when I think back over my months of hiding, I don't remember being afraid. It was just something I had to do. I was never particularly courageous—as I mentioned, I didn't join the Resistance—rather, I was simply unaware of danger. I traveled from Marseilles to Paris on a train crowded with refugees, people going to see their families, merchants, businessmen and the omnipresent German soldiers. If I had to hide out in the toilets during a document check, well, others were doing the same thing; if I had to hide between the cars from time to time, then I did so. This was not a show of heroics.

There was a moment of breath-holding when the Germans came through each car, but I was, after all, good at breath control. Several times during the journey the train stopped to get clearance and be searched. By late 1942 the Nazis had essentially taken over the whole country, but the checkpoints they had established were arbitrary, and I managed to stay one step ahead of the guards all the way. It was just part of what it took to get to Paris, and I needed to be in Paris. I arrived safely, if a little dirty and very tired, and found a hotel. I don't remember its name, because it was one of many I had to keep checking in and out of. Without the correct papers, my existence became necessarily nomadic.

My center of gravity was the Conservatory on rue de Madrid, near the Gare St.-Lazare in Paris's eighth arrondissement. Gaston Crunelle was surprised and happy to see me that January in 1944. He was aware that I didn't have the proper documents, but he also knew that I would be safe at the Conservatory, because its director, Claude Delvincourt, did all he could to protect his flock, never asking for papers and always trying to hide illegal students.

I had no fear of being turned over to the authorities, and though changing my hotel each week was a nuisance, it was nothing more than that. When I wasn't packing or unpacking, I had to study hard: I had only a week to spare before the midyear exam, and about ten difficult Paganini caprices to master. The midyear exams establish who can enter the annual Conservatory prize competition. I wanted to try for my first prize as soon as possible, to prove to both my father and myself that I was good enough. At the same time, however, I wanted to get back to Marseilles and be with my family. I did not know how long I could escape the attention of the Germans in Paris; I did not know what would happen. In a time without a future you do as much as you can in the present. I might never again have an opportunity to enter the competition.

I worked intensively during that first week and tamed Paganini to Crunelle's satisfaction. I had exactly four months to prepare for the annual competition.

Pierre Barbizet, my friend from Marseilles, and my father's musical contacts made it easy for me to feel welcome in the capital, despite the oppression of the Occupation. Barbizet was renting a room in a

large private house on rue Desbordes-Valmore in the sixteenth arrondissement, Paris's smartest neighborhood. It was a sort of musical
boardinghouse, occupied for the most part by Conservatory students
and run by a Madame Laurens Petit-Gerard, who was herself an
amateur pianist. The ambiance was pleasant, and we all felt at home.

It was not cheap, however, and Pierre's father constantly complained to mine that keeping Pierre in Paris was costing him more
than the deprivations of the war. He and my father figured that my
hotel-hopping, eating in restaurants and at the Conservatory canteen
came to less than what Pierre was paying at the boardinghouse, and
when Pierre's father arrived in Paris to try to persuade Pierre to
move, we decided we would find a place together.

Pierre was loath to leave Madame Laurens's, and in the end we
compromised; the "compromise" consisted of my moving in with
him and sharing the rent. The room was large enough for two beds,
and Madame Laurens was pleased with a new boarder who might
keep the unruly Pierre somewhat in check. Unlike his well-mannered
fellow students, Pierre was always late for meals, always on the
telephone, lunched in his pajamas and generally carried on like the
bohemian he was. My own habits were more socially acceptable—
after all, I had been practicing my Fred Astaire act for many years.
I packed my bags yet again and made the acquaintance of the musicians
at 5 rue Desbordes-Valmore.

The house has been torn down since then and replaced by modern
apartments, but I still live in the same neighborhood and continue
to remember with affection the musical amicability that reigned at
Madame Laurens's. It was there that I met Robert Veyron-Lacroix,
who was to become my dear friend and musical collaborator for more
than thirty years. When I first arrived, his position as an assistant
professor at the Conservatory and his more elegant single room placed
him miles above me, the new flutist. Though we were always cordial,
we did not immediately become friends.

It was at Madame Laurens's that I studied for the Conservatory
competition. There Pierre and I played far into the night, he muting

the piano and me fingering more than blowing. Yet we heard the music loud and clear all around us. The war brought its hardships—for us, this meant thin gruel rather than hearty food, and the depression of knowing we were a conquered nation—but it also brought a sense of clarity to the moment at hand, the day in one's life, the hour in that day, which heightened each and every experience. It taught me to live each moment as fully as possible despite the overwhelming sense of potential disaster.

I then made one final effort to exempt myself from military service and thereby earn the right to be living in Paris legally. I fixed an appointment for a medical checkup, hoping that I could somehow be stamped unfit for strenuous activity. I was on the lean side, but generally—and unfortunately for me—in very good health. A friend of Christian Bourde's father was a pharmacist in Paris, and Mr. Bourde arranged for him to give me some medication that would increase my heartbeat. I was to take it the night before the medical.

Panting and half dead, I arrived at the doctor's office in a state of near cardiac arrest. There was no way I could join the army.

"I'm Mr. Rampal, here to see the doctor," I gasped out to the nurse at the reception desk.

"Do you have an appointment?" she asked.

"Yes," I puffed.

"I'm sorry, Mr. Rampal, but the doctor has had to cancel all appointments for today. Can I reschedule you for tomorrow?" she said, smiling.

Another dose of that medicine would have killed me as surely as any German work camp. I left the doctor's office for good and retreated into the shadowy world of occupied Paris, where illegalities quite often passed under the noses of the Germans unnoticed.

*

The French may have given up the trenches without much of a fight, but many of them still continued to battle the occupiers. In Paris, a city that the Germans could administer but not completely control, people were nibbling away at the authorities in the back streets and under cover. My friend from Marseilles Herman Moyens, for one, was involved with a radio station in the rue du Bac. I was never exactly clear how it functioned; it did not have the official approval of the Germans, yet it made recordings and transmitted programs. Moyens had always been a master deceiver—even in his attempts to play music too difficult for his skills—and perhaps it was best that I didn't probe too deeply when he asked if I would make some recordings for him. He said they were for the American market and, because they were of outlawed Jewish composers, we would have to do them at night. I agreed.

The other musicians who showed up, all contemporaries of mine at the Conservatory, remained my dearest friends over the years. It was in the Club d'Essai one night in early 1944 that I first met oboist Pierre Pierlot, bassoonist Maurice Allard and clarinetist Jacques Lancelot. After the war, Pierlot, Lancelot and I would be joined by bassoonist Paul Hongne and horn-player Gilbert Coursier to form the Quintette à Vent Français, the French Wind Quintet. Pierlot, Hongne, Veyron-Lacroix and a violinist named Robert Gendre helped me form the Ensemble Baroque de Paris. Both these groups lasted fifteen or more years, and toured the world.

But that night back in 1944, it was a ragtag bundle of unknown musicians who converged on the little studio at rue du Bac after the curfew. We played works by Hindemith, Milhaud and Schoenberg. I never felt it was a risky thing to do—the only people who could have denounced us were the technicians, and they were all friends— and I didn't feel heroic, either.

I have always said that I was not particularly courageous during the war, but perhaps I was merely insouciant. I simply never saw the dangers clearly. After all, I was living without papers and illicitly helping to record works by outlawed composers. This was something we as musicians felt it was important to do at a time when most of our energy was being called upon for survival. It was a resistance of sorts. The tapes we made were shipped to America, but I am not sure who heard them, or when. For all I know they may be gathering dust on the shelves of some musical archivist, never to be heard again.

*

In wartime, food for thought was never a problem. Food for nourishment was a different matter, but I found a way to combine the two once a week at the house of Fernand Caratge, a great friend of my father, who, like my professor Gaston Crunelle, played the flute with the Opéra-Comique. Each Monday, on his day off from the Opéra, I would go to Caratge's house on rue Lagrange near Nôtre-Dame, and we would have both a musical and literal feast.

We would play duets in the afternoon and eat luxuries such as butter and eggs with our dinner. Caratge was giving lessons to a man who lived on a farm outside Paris, in exchange for food. I benefited both from his great musical knowledge and from his barter. Mondays at Caratge's set me up for the week.

Caratge and Crunelle formed a perfectly complementary pair of influences on my musical progress. They both played beautifully, but completely differently. Caratge had an integrity of style and a seriousness in total contrast to Crunelle's more elegant, poetic playing, which had both an allure and a chicness that was exciting. Caratge's approach was more scholarly; it had a subtle seriousness that was based on a deep understanding of musicology. It was Caratge who, after the war, encouraged me to research the flute repertories in the libraries of Paris and elsewhere.

It was also Caratge who might have put an end to my career as a flutist, though this thought hardly occurred to him when he voted against my receiving first prize in the year-end competition.

I had to play a very difficult piece by a contemporary composer, André Jolivet. Jolivet, thanks to Herman Moyens, was not new to me; I had in fact met him. Moyens had championed Jolivet years before in Marseilles, where I had performed his *Five Incantations* for solo flute at a private concert in 1941. When I arrived in Paris and went to play them for him again, he introduced me to the world of "La Jeune France," the group of composers Olivier Messiaen had first gathered around him in 1936. They were a generation older than I, but though I was never really a spokesman for contemporary music in France I remained close to the group and premiered many pieces by them, including four by Jolivet.

Jolivet's *Le Chant de Linos* was the commissioned piece for the 1944 flute competition at the Paris Conservatory. One other entrant, Paul Mule, the son of the famous French saxophonist Marcel Mule, and I played it from memory. I failed to win a unanimous vote: Mule and I shared the first prize. Caratge had cast one of the negative votes. My father later asked him whether my playing had been worse than that of any of the other contestants.

"No," said Caratge, "I just thought an extra year at the Conservatory would do him good."

I am sure that if I hadn't won first prize the first time around I would never have gone back and would have given up thinking about a career in music. My name would not have been known among the musicians in Paris, and after the war I would have returned to my medical training; no one would have thought to ask me to come back to Paris to play professionally. I probably wouldn't have cared. The severity of the war made my own conflict—the choice between music and medicine—seem unimportant. We would be lucky just to survive in one piece. Whether I became a musician or a doctor was irrelevant.

*

As time passed, however, I began to fear more and more for my family in Marseilles. I had decided that whether I won or lost the competition I would head back home as quickly as possible. And in May 1944 I had little time to celebrate my success. News was hard to come by, but there were rumors of major battles in Marseilles. Some people said whole sections of the town had been destroyed. Others even mentioned my own neighborhood. The Allies were moving in on the German troops, and I had to find out if my family was alive. The day after the Conservatory final I packed my bags and headed south.

This time the train journey, though long and arduous, presented none of the problems of my trek six months earlier. The Germans now had to watch out for more troublesome problems than illegal travelers. Finally, in the dead of night, we pulled into the Gare St. Charles in Marseilles. I started walking toward my home, my heart pounding. I knew the port had been badly bombed, but to my relief the tales of mass destruction appeared to have been greatly exaggerated.

I turned the corner toward rue Brochier: the street was still standing. I rang the bell at number 20, and my father came to the door. The family was alive and well. My first prize at the Conservatory was worth little compared to the joy of being home.

I stayed in Marseilles, and, as the summer of 1944 progressed, it became clear that the Allies were making progress. Membership in the French Resistance in France grew: more and more people began to believe in General de Gaulle's call for a Free France. The Germans bombed the area around the port, suspecting that that was where most of the Resistance fighters made their headquarters. Only the hospital was left undamaged. By now I had gone back to medical school, passed my exams and entered my third year of training, along with Christian Bourde.

There had been nothing else I could do. I might have stayed in Paris and continued with my music, but under what conditions? At that time there was no future for any of us in music. All the young men in France were living under false pretenses. We were supposed to have volunteered for the German work parties, but somehow or other, either by means of false papers or fabricated excuses, we had managed to escape. I didn't totally abandon music, but at that point in the war it was more expedient to be a doctor, so I put together a halfway legal existence, using my work in the hospital as a believable cover.

The summer of 1944 became, for me, a summer of tending patients in the Marseilles Hôtel-Dieu, the hospital, to which I would walk through the ruins of the old port. By now, instead of being totally resigned to the Occupation, we were once again starting to hope. News from the fronts was more encouraging: the Allies were winning in North Africa and the Russians had the Germans on the run in the east. We began to believe that the war might end soon, and that France would once more be free.

*

The French retook Marseilles on August 23, 1944. I remember that I was swimming at one of the beaches on the Corniche—Marseilles's coastal road—when the planes started to fly in. I heard several explosions from the port area, but it was all over so quickly I barely had time to dry myself.

The tumult of the Liberation was perhaps more dangerous in Marseilles than the war itself. The city had seen little fighting in the streets, but now violence erupted everywhere. Collaborators were hunted down, and rival Resistance groups sought to win power. At the hospital, we tended all the sick and wounded who came our way. And I managed to stay out of the crossfire.

In the months that followed, quiet once again came to Marseilles, and I was able to concentrate on choosing my medical specialty. I opted for urology—for me, a logical choice. One of my best friends, Jean Mirabel, who was two years ahead of me, was also a urologist, and I have always said if I was not playing with one pipe, I was bound to be playing with another. My first job was to assist the young doctors with IVs and minor operations. It was my first taste of what it was like to be a medical soloist. The operating room resembles a chamber ensemble, with skilled professionals all working together. Success depends on the harmony of the group as a whole. Chamber music doesn't have the same life-and-death imperative, but it does require the same element of understanding and expertise that must be present in an operating theater. I enjoyed the hospital work, and even though I had won my first prize at the Conservatory, I now considered myself back in the groove of a medical career.

But my friends in Paris were not going to let me escape that easily.

5

I Promise to Go Back to Medical School

"I PROMISE TO GO back to medical school after this concert," I told my mother as I left Marseilles for Paris in the spring of 1945. I had been invited to play the Jacques Ibert Flute Concerto with the Orchestre National de France.

"I don't need another musician in the family. I want a doctor," my mother replied, for the hundredth time that week.

My father said nothing. We never once discussed my decision to follow in his footsteps and try to establish myself as a musician. He knew there was little he could say, and I know he was proud of me. I was on the way to Paris for a prestigious engagement. Jacques Ibert had written his Flute Concerto for Marcel Moyse, the first great flutist of the twentieth century who had tried to establish the flute as a solo instrument. It seemed auspicious that I was following in his footsteps and playing a work he had premiered.

One concert does not make a musical career. It was a toss-up as to whether I would return to Marseilles and medical school or stay in Paris and play the flute. My promise to my mother was not made in bad faith, although I must admit that I harbored different hopes. As I took the train north, in the days when the war was still fresh in our minds and the final armistice had yet to be signed, I knew in my heart that I would never go back to medical school: it was merely a safety net, and one into which I did not want to have to fall. But I kept it there, as much to propel me forward as to allay some of my mother's fears.

My invitation from Paris came from two composers I had known in Marseilles, Henri Tomasi and Manuel Rosenthal. Tomasi, who was a friend of my father's, was born in Marseilles but considered himself Corsican and was probably the greatest composer and musical director ever to come from that island. I had met him through his father, Xavier Tomasi, who was an amateur flutist in a kind of "big-band" orchestra in Marseilles. Manuel Rosenthal, who in his youth had been one of Ravel's pupils, had told my father back in the days when I was still at the Lycée Thiers that he thought I was talented enough to have a major career in music and that he would help me if he could. He kept his promise when he was named director of Radio France after the war. At the time Henri Tomasi was conductor of the Orchestre National de France. Both musicians remembered me and knew that I had won my first prize at the Conservatory.

I went back to my room at the Pension Laurens and immediately looked up my friends from the Conservatory. I wanted to start playing with Pierre Barbizet, my friend from the Lycée Thiers. After I had won my prize and left Paris for Marseilles, I learned that Pierre had been caught and sent off to the work camps in Germany. I still had not heard from him, and the war was drawing to a close. After the Liberation, Pierre wrote a letter that described how he had hidden in a cellar during the fall of Berlin, but I wanted to see with my own eyes that he really was all in one piece. I also wanted to see Pierlot, Allard and Lancelot, my companions from the Club d'Essai nighttime recording sessions, as well as Herman Moyens, its director, who was now a producer with the French radio.

There was never a better time to be a young music lover in Paris, despite the fact that the city was still ravaged by the aftermath of war. The liberation of Paris, unlike that of Marseilles, had lasted several days, and much blood had been shed. The city had been torn apart in the conflict and was only slowly beginning to get back on its feet. I remember being there on Armistice Day, watching everyone dancing in the streets. It was so soon after my return to Paris that I hadn't had time to link up with my old friends, and I felt like a spectator rather than a participant. I knew I ought to feel happy that the war was over and that I had begun my career, but I was lost and temporarily friendless in a big city. The tears in my eyes were an honest mixture of joy for peace and sadness for my own solitude.

I needed to find the people I loved; in the end, that did not take very long. Madame Laurens's began to fill up with familiar faces. If Armistice Day itself is a sad memory, I also remember that the sadness didn't last. The orchestra season started again, and new chamber groups were sprouting up all over the place, like the burgeoning trees in the first warmth after a long, dark winter.

The world of entertainment was a much-needed antidote to the horrors of war and the continuing food shortage. The gruel at Madame Laurens's didn't seem to have improved much, and I was still as thin as a rake. It took a long while before food became more than a luxury. I remember in my early married days in 1947, a full two years after the war, my young wife still had a special youth ration book that allowed her two bananas a month. One month I ate two-thirds of her banana and her mother, who lived in the same house where we had an apartment, became incensed. "How could you do that?" she asked. "She's still growing!" And perhaps Françoise would have gained another inch with one more banana, but I must admit, I love her the way she is.

In 1945, with the Germans out of Paris, I was getting happier every minute. The beat to which the city marched was one dear to my heart. Baroque music captured the sentiment of the day. Bach, Haydn, Vivaldi & Co., with their precise, measured music, gave the public the security and sense of order that the war had taken away.

You knew where this music was going and what it would do. There were surprises in its elegance and beauty, but the emotions it evoked did not try to turn you inside out like the symphonies and concerti of the Romantics.

People were putting their lives back together, and the Baroque accompaniment fit the spirit of the day. For most people, it was a discovery of a rich new musical literature. I had begun collecting Baroque and Rococo musical scores before the war, but they were still not widely known. Now, as more music publishers started bringing out this "new" music, the public began to discover its wealth. That the Baroque era was also the golden age of the flute didn't hurt an aspiring flutist trying to see if there was a living to be made as a Pied Piper in postwar Paris.

My first radio concert under Henri Tomasi was a great success. Radio at that time was an extremely important medium for a musician. There were many live concerts and the stations would also record specific performances that would be relayed later. This was how we musicians could make money. Herman Moyens was one of the radio recording producers and he was always asking me to record for him; he had been intrigued by contemporary music when I first knew him in Marseilles, so it was not surprising that he should ask me to play pieces by living composers. In addition to the Baroque repertory, I remember recording Jolivet's *Five Incantations*—the same piece Herman had introduced to me in Marseilles when I was still a teenager.

The success and regularity of the broadcasts helped me establish myself on a firm financial as well as artistic footing in Paris. Given a few more concerts, and perhaps a record contract, I would be able to survive there long enough to see if I could make a career as a flutist. I still promised my mother I would investigate whatever it took to get admitted into a medical school in Paris, but in the rush of the music world I never got around to it.

*

Though we were constantly in touch with each other, Pierre Barbizet was no longer staying at the Pension Laurens. But we were old friends, musically well suited, and I had hopes of forming a concert duo with him. After all we had already been playing together for more than ten years.

The problem, as is often the case with young, highly strung artists, was women, and one woman in particular. Pierre had married a pianist and found himself run ragged at home. His wife did not take kindly to rivals for her husband's time. She also thought more of her career than his, though in my opinion he was by far the better pianist. He became a house-husband of sorts, and I could never rely on him to show up for a performance, let alone a rehearsal.

One night Pierre and I were scheduled to give a small recital for which we had barely practiced. I wasn't worried about that—we had worked on the pieces before—but I *was* worried that Pierre might not show up at all. I waited and waited. I tried to telephone him several times and finally he answered.

"We're supposed to play together tonight," I said. "Don't you remember?"

"I can't make it tonight. I just can't," he replied, exasperated. "I'm sorry but I just can't."

There was no use trying to persuade him. He would not show. What I needed now, in very short order, was a pianist to take his place.

Robert Veyron-Lacroix, a former acquaintance from the Conservatory and a brilliant pianist, lived two floors above me. He had won several prizes for solfège, music theory, accompanying and harmony, and was about to be given another award for piano. Unlike Pierre, who was a dark-skinned, Mediterranean type, Robert had all the refinement, style and reserve of a true upper-class Parisian. He was cultivated, precise, charming, very trim and very good-looking. I knocked on his door.

"I know this is short notice," I began, "but would you be free to play a concert with me this evening?"

I was met with a ready smile and twinkling eyes.

"What is it you want me to play, Jean-Pierre?" he asked. I explained the situation: Barbizet's family problems and the nature of the concert, which was to consist of several duets for flute and piano, a solo piece for flute and a solo for piano.

"You can choose whatever you'd like to play," I said, trying to be encouraging.

Robert took the scores from me and set them up on the piano he had in his room.

"Yes, I'm free this evening. Now, let's see what we have here," he said, as he started to sight-read.

And so began a relationship that lasted thirty-five years. As we raced through the music—there were only a couple of hours left before the concert—I realized that here was someone who complemented my own style of playing exactly. Though I was certainly closer to Barbizet in temperament, both of us being from Marseilles, I found in Veyron-Lacroix a perfect partner, even though we have completely different personalities. He is more refined and literary than I am, and takes a more controlled pleasure in elegance and elegant surroundings. I am more down-to-earth in the way I express myself and my enthusiasms.

As postwar Paris regained its chic, Robert took to the world of high society. He counted "jet-setters" among his friends, and was a regular guest at the elegant soirées organized by Marie-Blanche de Polignac. She favored small dinners for about twelve. The guests were always members of the artistic and intellectual elite, and the topics of conversation were decidedly refined.

For my part, I attended only one or two of these intimate evenings. I was put off by the *haute culture*, if I may call it that, and became a very shy fly on the wall. I barely entered into the conversation. Robert, however, has the witty, bantering type of personality that thrives in these situations. I am much happier in more relaxed surroundings; the tone may not be so lofty, but a friendly, down-to-earth atmosphere is much more entertaining for me.

Robert and I could, however, always agree on the way we liked to play music. His reserved, darker romanticism contrasted well with my more open and wholehearted approach, with the result that each tended to moderate the other's excesses, both on stage and off. Perhaps that is the key to our long collaboration. We enjoy the same things—good music, good food and good company—yet our approach to these pleasures is different. This was one reason why Robert himself never wanted to launch a career as a solo pianist: he was as much of a ham as I, as long as there was someone with whom to share the spotlight.

Our differences kept us together. Robert is my son's godfather, and he knows me as well as I know myself. As a reviewer once put it: we "breathed the music together."

From the very beginning we knew this could happen. Our initial rehearsal went just the way I like rehearsals to go, albeit on that occasion we were more rushed than usual. Neither Robert nor I plod through the music discussing every phrase; if you do that, you will never get from the practice room to the stage, because you will always have to stop to consider the next note. Robert and I didn't take a week to agree on an interpretation. We were already in agreement at the first run-through. We both sight-read very well, and we would often spend days playing all sorts of different pieces in order to familiarize ourselves with the repertory. Every work we decided to include in our repertory would be gone over carefully—but not a hundred times.

I am the same way with John Steele Ritter, who became my pianist in the late seventies after Robert started to have back trouble and retired from the stage. John, though completely different from Robert, has the same kind of working style: fast. He is from the American West, though he is not a frontiersman. His greatest joy, when he can spare the time from touring, recording and teaching, is to tend the garden in his Pasadena home. He is inherently very shy, and I think he would have been overcome with embarrassment if he'd had to attend one of Marie-Blanche de Polignac's soirées—just as I used to be. John also finds it hard to come to grips with a decision; he can hesitate for twenty minutes or so before deciding on what drink to order in a bar—in fact, I generally take over the ordering when we are traveling together. I let him deliberate over a menu for a while, but in the end hunger and impatience usually force me to help him make up his mind.

"Should I have this?" he always asks. "Or should I have that?"

"Mr. Ritter will take the swordfish and I will have the lobster," I tell the waitress as she comes around for the fifth time. And John will be happy. The burden of choice has been removed.

When it comes to musical interpretation, however, there are no delays. John is a wonderful musician who also sight-reads extremely well and who understands how I like to play. My interpretation is basically a classical one—something he picked up immediately—and we never argue as to where a certain emphasis should be placed. As with Robert, I feel that John and I share one voice when we are making music.

That first almost impromptu concert with Robert Veyron-Lacroix back in 1946 went extremely well. Barbizet continued to be unreliable, and Robert and I played together more and more. We began to establish a reputation for ourselves. For the first couple of years we performed in small concert halls and the occasional church or two; we even made a trip to Algeria to play with the French Radio Orchestra of Algiers. By the time Pierre settled down again and began to take his career in hand—following a divorce from his tempestuous wife—Robert and I were already a known duo and there was no question of my changing pianists. Barbizet later paired up with violinist Christian Ferras, and the two made a name for themselves touring around the world. Pierre is now the director of the Marseilles Conservatory; whenever my schedule permits, I return to our hometown to play. We still make a good duo, and I often wonder how our futures would have differed had we remained together in 1946.

*

When I think back to those early years in postwar Paris, my mind is something of a blur. Things moved extraordinarily fast. I started playing concerts with Robert, performed several times a month on the radio and joined numerous musician friends for chamber music concerts all over town.

One day I was in a studio on rue Armand-Moisant, near Montparnasse, recording the Mozart G-major Flute Concerto for the radio. Herman Moyens invited a friend of his, Levy Alvarez, to listen in. Mr. Alvarez owned a record store on the Boulevard Raspail called the Boîte à Musique, as well as a small, exclusive recording label of the same name.

The Boîte à Musique catalog represented Mr. Alvarez's personal taste: he simply recorded music that he liked. It was more of a hobby than anything else—he didn't need to earn money from selling his records. I was familiar with the list because at that time there was only a handful of recording companies, all of them, of course, making 78-rpm records.

After Mr. Alvarez heard me play the Mozart Concerto, he approached me with a suggestion: "I've decided to add the Mozart D-major Quartet for Flute and Strings to my catalog. I like the way you play Mozart. Would you be interested?"

"Why, yes, I would love to do that," I said, genuinely thrilled by the idea. It was my first contact with a recording company. "But with whom should I play it?"

"That's up to you," he replied.

Without hesitation, but with tremendous nerve, I decided to call on the best trio in Paris—perhaps one of the best in the world at that time: the Trio Pasquier. All three of the Pasquier brothers—Jean, the violinist, Pierre, the violist and Etienne, the cellist—were older than I, and I wasn't even sure if they would recognize my name. I called Pierre Pasquier, who managed the business end of the trio.

"This is Jean-Pierre Rampal. I am a flutist, and I was wondering if you might be interested in making a recording with me?" I said, as politely as I could.

I needn't have worried. "Ah yes, Mr. Rampal, I believe I have heard your name and your flute," Pierre Pasquier said. "Very good, very good indeed. Now what is it that you think might interest us?"

I explained Mr. Alvarez's proposition, which met with instant approval.

This was in the days when you recorded directly onto the wax master disc. You would rehearse a few bars for the sound engineer, and, when he thought he had the microphones in the right places, you would settle down to play an entire side in one fell swoop. You could not replay the recording without destroying the take: you either took the chance that the balance of sound was correct, or you listened to it and then had to throw out the master and start all over again.

We played the first movement extraordinarily well.

"I think that's all we have to do for that," said Mr. Alvarez happily. The sound engineer agreed.

"But suppose the balance is wrong?" I asked. "This is the very first record I've made. I'm not sure it will work."

"Perhaps you're right," said Pierre Pasquier. "Maybe we should check, just to be sure."

So we listened to the movement. The recording was terrific. There wasn't a single mistake. Unfortunately, once we'd listened to it we couldn't keep it; we had to rerecord the whole thing. Several hours and three or four attempts later we decided we'd better keep one of the versions.

"You know, we really should have . . ." a tired Pierre started to mutter.

"I know, I know, don't even say it," I interrupted. I was just as tired as he was, but had naturally been concerned that my first record should sound as good as it could. I don't think we ever matched that first take.

The record was a success, and the beginning of a wonderful friendship with the Trio Pasquier and the Boîte à Musique. Over the years I toured the world with Jean, Pierre and Etienne, and it is with great pleasure that I still tour and play with the Trio Pasquier—the trio now consists of two of Pierre's sons, Régis and Bruno, a fine violinist and viola player respectively, who decided to carry on family tradition and joined up with cellist Roland Pidoux to form the new Trio Pasquier.

Since that first early attempt, I have always loved to make records and have generally agreed to do so whenever my schedule permits. This has resulted in an enormous discography, one that I can't even keep track of myself. I must have recorded more than three hundred works so far, many with the finest musicians and orchestras of our time. I am only sorry that I have never been able to assemble a complete library of them. I have my favorites, of course, but all in all I think there are only about a dozen or so *navets* (turnips, as we say in French) or flops in the whole bunch.

A failure usually occurs when you don't get along with the musical producer; at that point, all you want to do is finish the recording and get out of the studio. It's like working with a conductor whose view of the music is totally different from yours. Ne'er the twain shall meet, and the end result will invariably sound tense and even a little angry. I've had such experiences, of course, but in general I am lucky. Over the years I have had the opportunity to work with some extraordinary producers and sound engineers, in particular Michel Garcin at Erato and Georges Kadar at CBS Records. Both men have sensed how I should sound on records and have managed to bring out all my best qualities.

For me, a musical producer has to be a friend, which is what both Georges and Michel are. People often ask how a performer can make a record without the presence of an audience, and I tell them that there *is* an audience, an audience of an extremely high quality: the producer, who knows your playing, your sound and your capabilities, and who believes in you. Let the producer be a good friend of mine and I have all the audience I need.

The producer plays the role of that special person in the audience to whom you have chosen to direct your playing. He must have a good ear and a good heart. He must know how to coax the best out of the musician, stop him when the playing falters, encourage him when the spirit weakens and calm his nerves when the score seems to have the upper hand. If a producer criticizes a musician too harshly or abruptly, and says things like "that's terrible; we can never release a record like that," the result is often the opposite of the one intended. The musician gets worse and worse.

There may be some people for whom this fierce approach works, but I'm not one of them. If I am criticized without a thought being given to my spirit, to my feelings, I have no wish to continue and would just as soon quit the studio or, for that matter, the stage. A good friend knows how to encourage you without destroying your morale. Michel and Georges are just such men, and I fear that records I have made with other producers do not match the quality of those I have made for Erato and CBS.

I am not the type of musician who is always dissatisfied with every take and never wants to release a single record. I believe that a recording captures one particular performance, one moment in time, and no more. If I do the best I can on the day I record, and if all goes well, then the record cannot help but be good. Some will be better than others, but that is often a matter of time and place.

Most recordings of classical music are not actually made in a studio, and I prefer to find places that capture the feel of a concert performance. This generally means that I have to record in a concert hall or perhaps a church. The only trouble with such settings is that it is impossible to control outside noises.

I remember about five years ago Georges Kadar chose a church in New Rochelle, New York, for a session with the Juilliard String Quartet. We were playing Friedrich Kuhlau's Quintets for flute and strings. Georges had tested the acoustics of the church's interior and found it resonant. The following week the Juilliard Quartet and I arrived, accompanied by a vast amount of recording equipment and a large number of technicians. In less than half an hour we realized that our task was going to be a difficult one. The wind had changed from the day when Georges had first visited the church, and we now found ourselves directly in the flight path of jets approaching La-Guardia airport, thirty miles away on Long Island. Every few minutes we had to stop what we were doing and wait for the *vroom* of a descending airplane to pass. Surprisingly enough, the result was a wonderful testament to the patience and professionalism of everyone involved. Neither I nor the Juilliard Quartet could afford to reschedule the session, so we did the best we could under the circumstances.

*

It seemed, those early days of recording in Paris, as if I just finished one session only to start another for a different label and in a different location in the city. Soon after my debut with the Boîte à Musique, the 33-rpm long-playing record was born, and with it numerous small recording companies. I was a young, unknown artist and only too pleased to offer my services whenever they should be required. I made records for L'Oiseau-Lyre, a high-class label started by an Australian music-lover named Louise B. M. Dyer. We always called her by her full name, rather like Cecil B. De Mille, for she was an impressive, opinionated woman who got intimately involved with the records she financed. In the beginning she took a dislike to Robert Veyron-Lacroix and insisted that I record with her own pet harp-sichordist. Then, just as suddenly and for no apparent reason, she decided Robert was wonderful after all, and that I *should* record with him.

I also recorded for labels such as Classic, which was started by Eddie Barclay, Discophiles Français and Ducretet-Thomson—names that have either been swallowed up by other companies or have quietly disappeared.

I made my very first recording in the early summer of 1946, and had to wait until the autumn before it was released. Working with the Trio Pasquier was a new experience for me, and it helped me to feel that I was now, finally, a professional musician, one whose life from then on would be totally involved with music making. I planned to send that first record to my parents to prove that, even though I hadn't found the time to enroll in medical school, my musical career was producing some positive results. As it turned out, I never did get to give it to them. That honor was reserved for a very important, very special new friend.

6

Taking
the
Cure

DURING THE WAR, THE Vichy I had known as the musical center of
my childhood summers had been transformed into the headquarters
of the French puppet government. This idyllic and romantic spa lost
its natural rhythm for several measures, but its heart, the natural
springs, still remained. In 1946 the Compagnie Thermale de Vichy
sought to return to the tranquil tempo of better times: there would
be a new season with a new orchestra. France itself was endeavoring
to take the cure after a long and difficult illness, and the powers
that reigned at Vichy decided to offer the old prescription of relaxation with musical accompaniment. It fell to a trombonist named
Joseph Alvizet to round up the one hundred or so musicians needed
to fill the bill.

Many of the older musicians in Paris returned to their jobs with
the various orchestras after the war. They were in no mood to travel.
The new crop of Conservatory graduates, however, jumped at the

idea: three months in a holiday resort, with lots of pretty young girls strolling along promenades simply waiting to be picked up by charming young musicians sounded just the ticket. When Alvizet came courting a wind section, he found Rampal, Allard, Pierlot, and Lancelot, the backbone of the newly formed Quintette à Vent Français, the French Wind Quintet, eager to please. We packed our bags and headed for the Gare Montparnasse posthaste.

For me, of course, Vichy held all the memories of a happy childhood, and even though I was leaving a fiancée behind in Paris, I was convinced that Vichy would, once again, provide a memorable summer.

My fiancée. Yes, like most of my contemporaries I had become a victim of the postwar engagement epidemic. People were tying knots and exchanging rings right and left. The freedom to think about the future inevitably spurred the nesting tendencies of the younger generation: marriage was the "in" thing to do, and I did not want to be left out. My fiancée was a beautiful girl named Hélène Achour, an old acquaintance from my dating days in Marseilles.

*

I have always loved women, it's as simple as that. As my wife, Françoise, says to this day: "Tall, short, round and thin; blonde, brown, black or brunette—you love them all." And, as I am not the shy and retiring type, I usually tell them so. If you can give a little pleasure, why not? Complimenting a pretty woman can make her smile, and complimenting a not-so-pretty woman can also make her smile—and then she appears much prettier. This approach has helped me make female friends all over the world. I am, after all, a Latin from a Mediterranean country.

I started testing my charms on ladies as a teenager of around sixteen or seventeen, and discovered that they worked. I would try to sweep young ladies off their feet with my manners and my English-cut suits, and it did seem that the girls liked me as much as I liked them. I would go courting quite often and found it far from arduous and generally very rewarding. After all, women sense when a man genuinely likes them. Since I was tall, not bad-looking and lively, I was never short of company.

One of the best ways to meet young ladies has always been to participate in some shared activity. As teenagers, Christian Bourde and I joined a local choir. Our voices contributed, after a fashion, to the tenor section, while our eyes contemplated the sopranos. Two lovely nightingales quickly caught our attention—Huguette Attal and Lil Achour. The choir gave concerts in and around Marseilles, and Christian and I were able to find seats on the touring bus next to our chosen songbirds. We flirted, of course, but respected the propriety of the times—it was, remember, 1941.

Christian fell in love with Huguette; I was infatuated with Lil. At the time I was interested in many girls, and found it hard to tell the difference between love and infatuation. That I could be strongly attached to more than one girl, however, made me think that I was not really in love, at least not to the extent that potential fiancés are supposed to be in love.

Lil was both extremely beautiful and extremely musical. She played the piano in addition to singing, and her passion for music mirrored my own. At the outbreak of war, when Marseilles began to be invaded with musicians and the Dominican church began its series of concerts-within-services, we were asked to contribute to the Sunday celebrations.

These were musically exciting times, but emotionally very traumatic. As the war progressed, the situation for the Achour and Attal families became increasingly difficult. The fathers of both our girlfriends were Jewish, and the Nazis were rounding up all the Jews—even those who were only half Jewish—throughout the city. Christian and I had had to say good-bye to Huguette and Lil when we left for the Chantiers de Jeunesse in 1943. Later in the year, by the time we had returned to Marseilles and gone into hiding, the situation had become even worse. Each week the Germans posted quotas listing the number of Jews to be deported. All my Jewish friends had fled to the country outside Marseilles. I had to leave and return to Paris to avoid being detained after defecting from the Chantiers, and my departure ended my relationship with Lil. Christian stayed in hiding in the South and, after the war, married Huguette.

Lil's father was captured and deported to Auschwitz, where he died. He was the only one I personally knew who was killed during the war. The Achour family, including Lil, and her two sisters, Hélène and Claudine, went into hiding and survived. After the war, Lil married Charles Deutsch, who, under the name of Charles Duployé, had been hidden by the Dominicans in Marseilles. He was the organist at the church in which we gave concerts, although none of us realized he was Jewish. He was a good composer and wrote many pieces for flute and piano which I used to play with Lil. Even though Lil survived the war, the tragedy of her father's death darkened her own passionate spirit; after the untimely death of her husband, she killed herself by jumping out of a window.

Following the Armistice, Hélène, Lil's younger sister, went to Paris to study singing. I had known her as the typical "younger sister of a girlfriend" in Marseilles, but she was now growing into a beautiful woman. We shared a love for music and a love for life. Paris had re-established itself as a city of pleasure; the restaurants and nightclubs had reopened and social life was beginning to return to normal. Hélène and I joined in the fun. When the marriage fever swept through Paris, we caught a mild case ourselves: I proposed to Hélène in the spring of 1946, and she accepted. I then packed my bags and left for Vichy with my companions. Hélène would have to wait for her ring until I returned.

Two days later, I started dating several of the young dancers from Vichy's resident company; I realized I was not in love with Hélène and that my bout of marriage fever was over. On my return to Paris in the autumn, I would have to reconsider my plans. I was by now sure that what Hélène and I felt for each other was not the kind of love that would be lasting; we were just good friends. I rather suspected that Hélène felt the same way. In the meantime, I found several new girlfriends in Vichy and had a tremendous, fun-filled summer. After all, I was only twenty-four—and, thank goodness, still a bachelor.

Toward the end of the season the orchestra scheduled the Mozart Flute and Harp Concerto. The harpist, who was known as Odette Le Dentu, came from Neuilly, near Paris. A week before the concert, she invited her seventeen-year-old daughter, Françoise, to visit. Odette and I held a rehearsal one afternoon, while Françoise listened from the back of the hall. When we had finished, Odette formally presented me to her daughter.

"Mr. Rampal, how well you play!" said Françoise.

"Why, thank you," I replied, puffing up like a strutting peacock.

"Actually, I don't really like the flute," continued the young lady.

"Oh?" I said, my chest instantly deflating.

"But you make it quite another instrument, Mr. Rampal. It somehow seems much louder, not just a peep from the middle of the orchestra."

A girl after my own heart—or so at least I hoped.

I immediately asked her mother if I could take Françoise boating the next day. And the day after that I asked if I could take her dancing.

Was it love at first sight? I'm not sure, but I know that I completely forgot my ballet dancers, Hélène, and all the other ladies I'd been so assiduously courting. I could think of nothing else but the petite brunette with the sparkling hazel eyes who, like her mother, played the harp.

That night on the dance floor, barely forty-eight hours after we'd first met, I took Françoise in my arms for the last waltz.

"If I weren't engaged already, I'd ask you to marry me," I said. I could hardly blame her if she didn't believe me, but I sensed something that wasn't just disbelief; it was more a kind of hesitancy on her part, a rather interesting moment of indecision. But, of course, a young Parisienne can hardly appear too eager.

"If I weren't engaged as well," she replied, apparently quite flustered, "I might have accepted."

With modest restraint we left it at that. I returned her to her mother, vowing to call her in Paris and to see her again. I had made up my mind, even if she hadn't. This was more than mere romantic infatuation. Françoise had touched something inside me that had never been touched before.

Back in Paris, I phoned Hélène and made a date for dinner.

"We have to talk," I said.

"Yes, we have to talk," she agreed.

Three months is a long time for two young people who are not really in love to be separated when there are other interesting young people around. And this time I was really in love. I was quite sure of it. When we sat down to eat, it was Hélène who started the conversation.

"Jean-Pierre, there's something I've got to tell you," she began.

"And there's something I have to tell *you*, Hélène," I echoed.

What a relief! Except that now I'd contracted an even worse case of the marriage bug, and this time it looked terminal. I phoned Françoise immediately; I had to make sure she'd call off her engagement then and there. I had just received the first copy of my first record, the Mozart D-major Quartet that I'd made with the Trio Pasquier, and I wanted to impress the love of my life and prove I was worthy of her sole attention. My parents would have to wait for their copy. It was the first present I ever gave Françoise.

To my delight, her suitor had mysteriously disappeared. My dance-floor proposal had so flustered Françoise that all she'd been able to do was to repeat my own words back to me. In fact, there *was* no "fiancé"—I didn't have to win her away from anyone. But as it turned out, my task was even more difficult. Françoise's father had died when she was very young, and her grandfather had taken over the role. It was he I had to win over—a loving and extremely protective grandfather, who had in mind a solid professional—a banker, doctor or lawyer, perhaps—as a husband for Françoise.

Before I could even set foot in the house at Neuilly I had to provide character references from Marseilles. I wrote my father, who duly prepared a note of recommendation, though he also made sure to put me in my place.

"Aren't you being a bit fickle, Jean?" he mused. "You start the summer with one fiancée and you end it with another."

My reputation as a ladies' man always amused him. He wondered just how serious I was going to be this time.

"This is the real thing, I promise you."

A formal and very stiff luncheon was arranged at Françoise's grandparents' house. It made me considerably more nervous than any musical audition would have done. Françoise had obviously told her grandparents how much she wanted me to continue my courtship, and I had made my honorable intentions clear to her mother, Odette, who was, thank goodness, on my side.

Grandfather eyed me most carefully on my arrival. He may have been as nervous as I was. He was looking at a rival for his granddaughter's attention, one he was afraid would take her away. The strain proved too much. On the way into the dining room he stumbled and fell. I was at his side before the family could take another breath. After all, I'd completed three years of medical school and a stint at the Marseilles hospital. I loosened his collar, prescribed a little brandy and got him to his feet. To this day Françoise swears that my swift action and obvious concern won the heart of my future in-laws. The wedding was set for June 7, 1947.

The rain that morning threatened to ruin the day. When the bride arrived, an avenue of umbrellas had to protect her, her white dress and the bridesmaids as they entered the church. But in the time it took us to say our vows, the clouds departed, and we had sunshine to warm us on our way back to the grand reception at Françoise's grandparents' house. Despite the lingering food shortages, my new family managed to put on a magnificent feast for the hundred or more wedding guests. After the banquet, we left for ten days in the Normandy countryside and then returned to Paris to set up an apartment—in Françoise's grandparents' house. As I had told her grandfather, I had no intention of taking her away. Family is sacred to me. By marrying, you enlarge a family, you don't just start a new one. I wanted to move into my wife's family quite as much as I wanted her to move into mine.

We had barely settled down before the summer arrived and I was once more engaged by the Compagnie Thermale de Vichy. With the memories of war finally beginning to fade, love was as tangible as the air, and glorious food was once more appearing in the shops. I gave myself over wholeheartedly to the experience. In the frenzy of happy indulgence that so often follows hardship, I decided it was time for me to gain a little weight. In fact, Pierre Pierlot and I were so intent on this new regimen that by the time we headed back to Paris we were both quite solid reflections of our former shadowy selves.

We returned to Vichy the following year, 1948. This time, a new member of the family was on the way. As Françoise's body began to grow, I, enjoying a second summer of abundance, grew right along with her. Shortly thereafter, Isabelle was born and Françoise regained her normal size. Not me, though. From then on I have maintained a somewhat portly appearance—what we in France call *important*. Françoise does try to make her husband a little less *important* from time to time, but what can you do when you love life—and food— as much as I do?

This may be the only battleground on which Françoise and I cross swords. I knew from the first moment I saw her that I had met my true love, and I was right. She has been and still is the backbone of my life. She manages me and my affairs today just as she has done from the very beginning. I have no idea where I would be without her. I may like them all—the tall women, the short, the blonde and the dark—but it is my petite brunette who captured and keeps safe my heart.

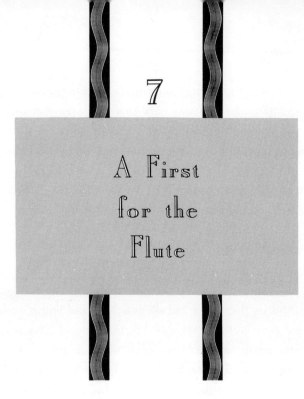

7

A First for the Flute

ONE OF THE THINGS that most impressed Françoise from the very beginning was the fact that I was absolutely convinced of what my aim in life would be: I wanted to make the flute a solo instrument, one that would rank alongside the violin and the piano. Sitting in a little rowboat on a lake in Vichy, I told her this firmly and with great conviction, and I never for one moment believed it to be anything but entirely possible.

You might say that my desire to be a solo instrumentalist propelled me to believe that the flute should become an instrument of solo rank. The flute itself was important only in that it happened to be the instrument I knew how to play. The music came first, and my love of playing. Now I would have to start making sounds on the flute that would put both me and my instrument in the spotlight.

The biggest problem was to convince the public that the flute could be a solo instrument as credible as the piano. Nobody gave flute recitals at this time. Consider Marcel Moyse: between the wars, he had established himself as the preeminent flutist of his generation. He made many records and gave numerous concerts, but primarily he played with his daughter-in-law, Blanche Honegger, a violinist and viola player, and his son Louis, a pianist, as part of the Trio Moyse. Though Moyse also made solo recordings and definitely established a tradition for the solo flute, he rarely took the stage alone. Still, Moyse did make one consider the possibilities: he unlocked a door that I continued to push open.

I never studied with Moyse, though he did influence me considerably. He was not teaching at the Conservatory during the war, and, when he returned afterward, I had already received my first prize and begun my career. At first, he seemed to hold this against me. He had tremendous respect for my father—Moyse had been one of the judges on the board of his Conservatory entrance audition in 1913—and whenever the name of a flutist called Rampal came up, he immediately thought of Rampal *père*. When he was told that the conversation referred to Rampal *fils*, he would say, "Ah, you mean the doctor," as if he didn't think I took the flute seriously. We talked about this later, when Moyse was much older, and he came to realize that it was not necessary for me to have studied with him to be influenced by his playing.

Moyse's style was very different from my father's. He attacked the flute with a force that was almost bellicose. I only heard him once in concert, toward the end of his career, and he impressed me with the strength with which he played. He emphasized the power of the flute with every breath he took, making the audience sit up and take notice of his fragile silver pipe.

Despite his popularity, Moyse never tried to make a career of flute recitals. A flutist might play a solo piece on a program with a string quartet, but a whole evening of nothing but flute music was almost unheard-of. In fact, I remember attending only one such recital. It was given by Maurice Werner, a Swiss flutist, just after the war. Werner did not possess the messianic zeal of a true Provençal *cabotin* and eventually gave up the flute in favor of becoming an impresario.

If anyone could change the way people thought of the flute, I was sure it would be a Frenchman. Various instruments often seem to become identified with specific countries—Israel and the violin, for example—and wind instruments are almost a tradition in France. Without doubt my personal style has always been very nationalistic. I come from a long line of French flutists and from a city that has played its own part in a history that began long before the Rampals took to the instrument. One of the greatest known flutists, Pierre Gabriel Buffardin, who was born at the end of the seventeenth century, came from Marseilles. After a stay in Constantinople, as it was called then, he went to Dresden, where he played with the Dresden Orchestra. There was a German oboist in Dresden at that time named Johann Joachim Quantz, whose whole life was changed by Buffardin's playing. He gave up the oboe in favor of the flute, and started to study under Buffardin.

Quantz, a German, wrote one of the best treatises on the flute: *Versuch einer Anweisung, die Flöte traversière zu spielen* (*Essay on a Method for Playing the Transverse Flute*). This was published simultaneously in French and German in 1752, and I am lucky enough to have an original copy. Quantz's description of the perfect flutist still holds good today. "The spirit," he wrote, should be "lively and fiery, united with a soul capable of tender feelings; a good mixture without too much melancholy. . . ." The body should be "completely healthy . . . [with] strong and open lungs; prolonged breath, even teeth that are neither too long or too short; lips that are thin, smooth and delicate rather than puffed out and thick . . . a fluent and skillful tongue; well-formed fingers that are neither too long nor too short, too corpulent or too pointed but are provided with good tendons, and an unobstructed nasal passage for inhaling and exhaling easily."

In 1728, Quantz became the teacher of Frederick the Great at his court in Berlin. Frederick adored the flute and was a player of considerable skill, giving much time and effort to enlarging and improving the repertoire; to my mind, however, he does not seem to have been deeply moved by the music itself. When he lost his teeth and could no longer play, he also lost interest and ceased to be a patron of music at the court. I am not even convinced that he himself composed all the two hundred or more pieces attributed to him. Much of what he wrote was undoubtedly corrected and edited by Quantz: just how much is unknown. Quantz did, however, succeed in making Berlin a center for the flute, and his contact with Buffardin ensured that the French influence continued.

Although the traditions endured, the actual instrument changed. The flute for which Bach, Vivaldi and Mozart composed was little more than an awkward pipe. It could not play an entire chromatic scale, and it required an adept musician to keep the sound regular. However, it was relatively easy to master the basics, and toward the latter part of the eighteenth century flutemania took hold of Europe. The instrument became an entertainment in and of itself. Philip Bate reports in *The Flute*, his history of the instrument published in the early part of this century, that in 1776 an equestrian named Mr. Coningham advertised in London that as part of his performance he would ride two horses while playing the flute—all at the same time.

But showmanship was not the point. Flutists and flutemakers were now trying to find a way to give each chromatic semitone a finger-hole of its own, thus making the instrument more flexible and adaptable. By the end of the eighteenth century, however, even the most advanced flute had only eight keys. There was no consistency in the development process, and each flute was different, depending on the flutemaker and the region from which he came. Though more mechanization was added from year to year, the shape of the flute remained standard. They were all conical bore, tapering slightly from the foot to the head.

The breakthrough came in the early nineteenth century, when Theobald Böhm, the son of a Munich goldsmith and jeweler, started tinkering around with the instrument. Böhm was a good flutist and a master craftsman, and he was dissatisfied with the flute he owned. In 1810, after he had been lent a four-keyed instrument, he made a copy of it. He was still dissatisfied with the sound, particularly with the discrepancies between the upper and lower registers, and determined that there had to be a better solution.

Böhm played with the Munich court orchestra during the day and at night continued to reinvent the flute. By 1828 his efforts had gained so much popularity he decided to found his own flutemaking factory. He was by then a virtuoso flutist, and his travels during the next few years took him to London, where he was forced to admit that the sonority achieved by the flutist Charles Nicholson (1795–1837) was rounder and larger than his own. On analyzing the Englishman's flute, Böhm realized that the large size of the finger-holes was a major contributing factor. He also realized that unless one had truly gigantic fingers the only way to cover these holes would be by means of a highly complicated key system.

In 1832, Böhm started manufacturing a new kind of flute which he had designed on returning from London. It was a work of craftsmanship as much as design. The finger-holes were now opened and closed by keys mounted on gold pillars, which had springs that were also made of gold. The "Böhm system," as it came to be called, was a major improvement, but it failed to win over all the flutists of the period because it required totally new fingering. After a decade or so, Böhm decided to try again; he began working with an acoustician named Karl Franz Emil von Schafhäutl, testing the acoustics of the standard conical flute. He eventually produced a new shape for the instrument: a cylindrical bore. (This was not a truly new invention, however: the recorder, which was an earlier form of the flute, had a cylindrical bore which was later changed to a conical bore.) Böhm also added four additional keys to make up the chromatic scale, which necessitated an even more elaborate mechanical system.

In 1847 Böhm fine-tuned his design and exhibited his models in both London and Paris. In 1851 he won a patent for the "Böhm system," and in 1855 won the design-of-the-year award at the Paris World's Fair. Controversy continued to surround the "Böhm system," however. The English maintained that Böhm had stolen his design from a Mr. James Gordon, who was, it is true, working on a similar model. (Mr. Gordon—who was sometimes erroneously known as "Captain" Gordon—was rather a fascinating character; he was born in Cape Town, South Africa, traveled widely, and died insane in

1845.) In any event, the French flutemakers started licensing the Böhm model almost immediately, producing several variants of it. Master craftsmen like Clere-Godefroid, Rive and Louis Lot were responsible for perfecting the Böhm flute.

The flutes we use today are contemporary models based on the "Böhm system." They each have sixteen keys and three sections: the *head*, which includes the mouth or embouchure of the instrument; the *body*, which has thirteen holes (covered by keys) that produce most of the scale. The third part of the flute is the *foot*, which has three more holes, covered by keys, controlled by the right-hand little finger.

All but one of my flutes were made in this century. The other, my prize possession, dates from 1869. I came across this particular flute, which became a sort of good-luck symbol for me, my *flûte en or*, at the end of 1948, quite by chance. During that summer I had made the acquaintance of Gabriel Dussurget, the director of the Bureau de Concerts de Paris and the man who helped arrange my first solo recital, and a friend of his, Henri Lambert, an antiques dealer. One day Lambert mentioned to me that he had bought a golden flute some time after the war and planned to melt it down. The flute, he said, was made in China and came from Shanghai.

I was immediately interested, but very much doubted that anyone in China had ever made a gold flute. I had, in fact, heard of a golden flute that had been made in France in the nineteenth century by Louis Lot and then been exported to China, but the story had always seemed more like rumor than truth.

Lambert disagreed. "Yes, this must be it," he said. "It was made for the Comte de Rémusat."

He has always persisted in telling everyone that the flute I bought from him had been custom made for the Comte de Rémusat. Lambert was the kind of antiques dealer who loved spreading little anecdotes of this kind about the things he sold, and though I repeated time and time again that the flute was actually built for a *Monsieur* Jean Rémusat, the media always reports that I played the *comte's* flute. Jean Rémusat was not of royal birth, just a mid-nineteenth-century flutist who, at the end of his career in France, accepted an appointment as president of the Shanghai Philharmonic Society. Gratified, its members commissioned Louis Lot to make him a golden flute.

Before Lambert showed me the instrument—or what he said was the instrument—in 1948, I could not imagine what it was. What he handed me resembled a flute as much as a bag of bones resembles a skeleton. But at the first look, I knew that it was "the gold Louis Lot." All the pieces would have to be reassembled before I could tell if it would really amount to anything; I wasn't even sure if it was all there. Still, I took the bag of gold "junk" to Marseilles to get a second, expert, opinion.

My father was so excited at the idea that we might have the only gold flute made by Louis Lot that he stayed up all night putting the puzzle together. We ended up being extraordinarily lucky. Though the flute had traveled far and wide in its century-long life, it slowly became clear that nothing was missing. By morning, the flute had been completely restored to its original glittering condition.

Henri Lambert was not particularly impressed by the esthetics. He refused to let me buy the flute outright—he had, after all, wanted it for the metal, the gold, and it was gold he wanted in exchange. The flute, which weighed just over a pound, was made of eighteen-carat gold. Lambert demanded a pound's worth of napoléons (twenty-four-carat gold coins) in exchange. It was only three years after the war, and that kind of money was not easy to come by, but Françoise's grandfather pulled all the strings he could and we eventually handed over Lambert's pound of gold.

I know I got the better part of the bargain: there is only one gold Louis Lot, and it is the Stradivarius or the Del Gesu of all flutes. As I have said, I played this flute for eleven years and only retired it when I was presented with a contemporary gold flute by Lola Haynes of William S. Haynes & Co., the Boston flutemakers.

There will always be an argument about which metal produces the best flutes. Some studies have reported that the metal used makes no difference, but my own preference is obvious: I find the sound of a gold flute particularly warm. If you have a naturally sparkling sound, a gold flute enhances it and makes it richer; it gives you more colors, more shading. If you do not have a naturally sparkling sound, it is perhaps best to play a silver flute. To my ear, the sound of a silver flute is more brilliant and can help to enliven the playing, although I find it lacks the depth and roundness of a gold one. Personally, I have never been a fan of platinum, either in flutes or in jewelry. I find that it has a dull sound, and, moreover, is heavier. A platinum flute weighs two hundred grams—about seven ounces— more than a gold or silver flute, both of which weigh about the same. Although two hundred grams might not sound like very much— especially to a man who can demolish two hundred grams of almost anything in a couple of mouthfuls—playing a platinum instrument for several hours a day can become tiring.

I remember once playing a famous platinum flute that had belonged to Julius Baker, the first-chair flutist with the New York Philharmonic. The flute was a sturdy instrument that had been made for him by Vernon Powell, a former craftsman at William S. Haynes & Co. who had left to start his own workshop. Baker loved this flute, and I must admit it was beautiful, but he gave up playing it because it was too heavy and tiring. He sold it to Samuel Baron, who enjoyed playing it for a while, but who also rejected it as being too heavy.

I have stayed with gold flutes for forty years, and only stopped playing the Louis Lot when I began to worry about its being stolen. It is irreplaceable, and I feel less anxious knowing it is under lock and key. The last time I used it was for a recording of Bach's Fifth Brandenburg Concerto with the Academy of St. Martin-in-the-Fields, conducted by Neville Marriner. We made the record in London, and, as I was going there just for the day, I decided to take one rather than two flutes. I took the Louis Lot. It was a marvel, a truly precious thing.

*

The good news about the nineteenth century was that it saw the most advances in flute design; the bad news was that the nineteenth century also witnessed the steepest decline in the quality of music written for the instrument. The great composers of the period ignored the new developments. Except for a few pieces by Schubert and an early Sonata for Flute and Piano by Beethoven, there is little important nineteenth-century flute music. I think it is because the flute virtuosi of the time also became the officially recognized composers for the instrument. Unlike today, where the gap between performers and composers is rarely bridged, the nineteenth-century performer was tutored in composition and considered himself as much a composer as an instrumentalist. Unfortunately, the flutists/composers of the last century were overly preoccupied with the newfound flexibility of their instruments, so that the tendency was to extend the virtuoso limits of the new system rather than to compose music memorable for its depth or beauty.

The result was a superfluity of showpieces. It was hard for anyone to take the flute seriously. The great Romantic composers, such as Brahms and Schumann, devoted their energies to the piano and the violin, or to even newer instruments such as the clarinet, which offered them a chance to explore a new degree of sonority. To them the flute was merely a device on which virtuosi played series after series of constantly spiraling notes in the style of an operatic diva.

The early twentieth century saw a keener interest in the flute among composers, and the resurgence of more innately musical flute virtuosi. These included Moyse, who remained in France, and his contemporary Georges Barrère, who took the French flute school to America after World War I. His trademark, in addition to a superb musical talent, was one of the first platinum flutes. Barrère was able to gain the attention of his audience and, at the same time, follow in the footsteps of the true French tradition of flute playing. His students ranked among America's most-beloved flutists, and included William Kincaid, who in turn passed on the French tradition to today's generation of flutists such as Julius Baker and Samuel Baron— the teachers of the next generation.

Is there any difference between a French flutist and a player from somewhere else? There once was, but with the advent of recordings and global marketing the distinctions are blurring. There *have* been great differences, especially between the French and Germans. The German school could be described as having a heavier sound than the French, with a ponderous staccato and no vibrato—that peculiarly light and especially French flutter of a sound. Germans played with the tongue pressed more firmly against the teeth; this produces a thicker sound. The French only brush the back of the teeth with the tongue, and the sound is much lighter.

This effect is probably brought about by the different ways in which the two languages are spoken. German is hard and guttural, whereas French is more delicate and uses the muscles in the front of the mouth. I used to think that you had to speak French in order to play the flute well, because the muscles developed while speaking influence the sound made when playing. Now I believe it is only a matter of *how* you are taught to play. And with the internationalization of music—touring teachers, recordings, tapes—everyone is taught in pretty much the same way. Gone are the days when you could tell, instantly, whether a Japanese flutist had been taught by a French-man, an American or a German.

*

I had no desire to break with the tradition of French flute playing. I simply wanted to bring that tradition to the attention of more people. I had no set plans on how to achieve my goal, though, looking back, I see that certain events put me on the right path.

My first major recital in Paris was clearly an important move in that direction. It came about through my own initiative and with the help of my wife's grandparents.

Robert Veyron-Lacroix and I had been giving concerts and making recordings all over Paris, and I felt sure we could command an audience in one of the major concert halls. I did not have a manager or an impresario at that time, but I did have a supportive family who believed in me. Together, we decided to take matters into our own hands. My grandparents-in-law put up the money, and I approached Gabriel Dussurget at the Bureau de Concerts de Paris. We reserved the Salle Gaveau for Wednesday, March 9, 1949. The room, which is still used today, holds 1,500 people. We hoped we could "warm" half the seats, our break-even point.

From a very early age I used to fantasize about programs for flute recitals, even before there was any real chance that I might have to choose one. My thoughts generally ran along the same lines as those of a violin soloist: sonatinas—shorter pieces—wrapped around a major sonata. The key for our debut recital was to find a mix that would interest a public unaccustomed to spending an entire evening in the company of just a flute and a piano.

For months, Robert and I raced through the repertory available for flute and piano and started putting together a substantial library of possible pieces. Making the right decision about what to play at our first major recital was vital. I think I have a flair for programing— a talent that is very important to the success or failure of a solo career. I have also been fortunate in knowing people who think along the same lines as I do, and friends who know composers anxious to write interesting music for me.

For the Salle Gaveau concert, we decided on a tasty menu that brought together both the very new and the familiar; then we added a couple of little hors d'oeuvres to catch people's attention.

"We should definitely include Bach and Mozart," said Robert, as we started to list the ingredients.

Both of us knew our audience well. The Parisian public is drawn to those composers it loves, and you cannot go far wrong with a bit of Bach for flute and harpsichord, and then some Mozart, perhaps solo piano music. These would be morsels guaranteed to please.

Then I decided to do some digging.

"Do you remember that piece by Beethoven I turned up in the library?" I asked.

"The sonata for flute and piano, the one he wrote when he was thirteen?"

"Yes, that's the one."

"It isn't the most profound piece of music," Robert complained, raising an eyebrow.

"I know. But I don't think it's been played in public before, at least not for a very long time."

I had come across this tidbit while poring through the catalogs at the Bibliothèque Nationale. Though it was interesting in a historic sense, I agreed with Robert about its musical worth. Nevertheless, it would be sure to intrigue the critics if no one else, and we were hoping to get a review or two.

"And the Prokofiev to follow that," I added.

We both agreed that this would be the main course. The piece had been premiered in Moscow during the war, but had never been performed in France. A premiere is always good programing: the public likes to be involved with a first.

"Shouldn't we have something French?" asked Robert.

"Of course, but what?"

I shouldn't have needed to stop to think. The very person who had helped me to launch my career by asking me to perform the Jacques Ibert Flute Concerto had written a Sonatina for flute alone, which he wanted me to premiere. What better place than the Salle Gaveau?

"I have to do Henri Tomasi's Sonatina," I declared.

We rehearsed the pieces and found that the assortment made an entertainingly eclectic combination. The public would come because they were familiar with Bach and Mozart, and then they would be delighted to discover the newness of Prokofiev and Tomasi. Ever the eternal optimist, I couldn't see any reason why we wouldn't be wildly successful. There were, of course, nay-sayers, who insisted the public wouldn't show up and that I was crazy to think an evening of flute music would draw anyone beyond my own family and friends.

Robert and I didn't have eight hundred and fifty friends or relatives between us, and we didn't give away tickets on street corners, but that's about how many people showed up that blustery March evening. The hall was more than half full, and we felt we'd pulled off a tremendous success. My in-laws didn't lose money, and, though I don't think we earned much, I had made my point. We went home to celebrate and, as usual, Françoise, in what was to become a family tradition, put on a wonderful party for my friends. The verdict was unanimous: a flute recital could attract a paying public. But what would the critics say?

The reviews started appearing. They were extremely favorable, and although they didn't make front-page headlines, we were commended as much for our playing as for the careful, clever programing. The *Figaro* even went so far as to say that those who didn't go had missed a rare musical event. Little did I realize that this was just the first step on what was to be a long, long road.

8

The Wine Quintet
and the
Barrel Ensemble:

Making Music with Friends

ROBERT AND I HAD launched one part of our musical careers. We soon discovered that there was an audience for flute and piano recitals, but we also knew that you couldn't give such recitals every week. Like my father before me, I would have to cobble together a variety of musical jobs in order to earn a living. I had a few recording contracts and some radio engagements on my schedule, and I had also started playing more and more chamber music.

A chamber music ensemble is a wonderful environment for a musician who adores being a soloist but who also greatly enjoys making music in the company of his friends. And, for me, making music with my friends is as important as making music itself. Being in such close contact with people you love somehow brings out the very best in the music you love. It's something I've always done, from the early days in the Chantiers de Jeunesse barracks to my solo debut with Robert Veyron-Lacroix and to my most recent recordings with Isaac Stern and Slava Rostropovich.

The harmony of friendship translates perfectly into the harmony of music, chamber music in particular, for here you have a group of soloists each playing a separate part: it can only work as a whole if the group plays with the same spirit. If you don't love the people you play with, playing chamber music stops being interesting. Among others mentioned in this book, I have had particularly enriching experiences performing chamber music with the Juilliard and Guarneri Quartets, Jaime Laredo, Sharon Robinson, Anthony Newman, Julius Baker, Eugenia Zukerman, András Adjorán, Michaela Paetsch, Trevor Pinnock, Leslie Parnas and Shigenori Kudo.

To be a good chamber musician you have to be a very accomplished artist yourself, and in addition you have to have the ability to inspire those you are playing with. Alexander (Sasha) Schneider, for example, is such a strong personality and such a great musician that when you play with him—even if you don't exactly agree with his interpretation of the music, the tempi or the accents—you play the way he leads. He is the leader among leaders.

Sasha is one of the greatest musical personalities I have had the good fortune to know. If you mention Sasha, everyone knows whom you're talking about. It's the same for Isaac and Slava.

Apart from his great talent as a violinist and a musician, Sasha is a wellspring of memories and recollections. I could listen to Sasha the raconteur for days on end. And if he doesn't sit down and record all his stories one day, I may be forced to lock him in a room with a tape recorder myself. I wouldn't presume to tell any of his favorites here, that's for him to do,* but his special Jewish humor is the kind that always doubles me up with laughter. Maybe that is why I'm such a fan of Groucho Marx and Woody Allen. I am only happy that I have been able to share some of Sasha's musical experiences with him. Some of his culinary ones, too, for that matter, because Sasha

---

* Just before this book went to press, I received a copy of *Sasha: A Musician's Life*. Bravo, Sasha!

is a superb gourmet. The two skills go well together—rather like the harmony of chamber music.

One of my most moving chamber music experiences was in Toronto in 1987, when Walter Homburger retired as general manager of the Toronto Symphony Orchestra. He decided to celebrate his retirement in a way that would benefit the orchestra and asked many of his friends if they would be available to play—and almost all of us were.

Isaac Stern, Pinchas Zukerman, Slava Rostropovich and I readily agreed to go to Canada to play a little chamber music. We performed the Mozart Quartet in D major for Flute and Strings in a live radio broadcast, with Pinky taking the viola part. The synergy and energy that we generated was extraordinary. We took our cues from one another and entered completely into the spirit of the music. Unfortunately the concert was never captured on disc, but it did inspire us to make a recording. When we next got together Pinky could not be there, so Salvatore Accardo took his place. Slava, Isaac and I have so enjoyed recording together that now we are constantly looking for open dates in our schedules in order to make more records.

That mixing of musical minds was but a continuation of my lifelong love for chamber music. After the war, I had the chance to be part of two particularly fine groups. One, the French Wind Quintet— the Quintette à Vent Français—was started by my old friend the oboist Pierre Pierlot in 1946. Although at first sight Pierre may appear rather shy, he has an extraordinary sense of humor and a love for life that is wholly infectious. When he asked me to join him, clarinetist Jacques Lancelot, bassoonist Paul Hongne and the horn player Gilbert Coursier, I was more than delighted.

I consider the Quintette à Vent Français to have been one of the best chamber groups of its time. We played and toured together for more than fifteen years, attaining a standard of excellence I often found myself marveling at. We had an affinity for music that went far beyond the written notes, and I only wish that the repertory available to such a group had been a little more commercial.

The joviality and the friendship between us brought an extra dimension to the music. Pierlot, Lancelot, Hongne and Coursier were masters of their instruments. Pierlot was building up a library of solo works for the oboe. Our bassoonist, Hongne, was an intuitive musician who, despite the fact that he had never received much formal education, played his instrument with an intelligence and depth that presumed an innate sense of life and culture. When he was parted from his instrument he tended to be on the gruff side, but as soon as he started to play he became a great artist.

Jacques Lancelot, my friend from the Club d'Essai days in Paris, was a true clarinet virtuoso. His subtle style and dexterity opened my ears to the special sound a clarinet can produce. He used a light vibrato, something I had never heard before on a clarinet. The horn player in the Quintette, Gilbert Coursier, was also a virtuoso. He could produce a warmly colored, especially round tone that blended well with the differing timbres of the reed instruments and the flute.

When I listen to our old recordings and remember our concerts together, I cannot say that I have ever played with a better group.

I am sure that the unique combination of our different personalities enriched our music making. Pierlot, whose sense of punning repartee was as sharp as Lancelot's, would tease and make fun of us for days at a time. Hongne, who was a little naïve, would often take the two quite seriously, which would reduce Gilbert Coursier and me to helpless laughter.

We all had a great fondness for fine cuisine and for the good life—perhaps too great a fondness. Pierlot took to calling us the Quintette à Vin Français—the French Wine Quintet. Not that we were in our cups all the time; we just knew how to enjoy ourselves. There was never a time on our tours, especially those abroad, when we were bored, even for a moment.

I remember one occasion, however, when we almost came to blows. It was during a tour of northern France, and by the end of the first week we had almost decided to call it quits and disband. For some reason, Pierlot and I had started having fits of laughter onstage, often so bad that they almost prevented us from playing. I had only to catch his eye, or he mine, and we were convulsed. Lancelot wouldn't be far behind, and Coursier, too—only Coursier tried not to let his laughter show and played musical jokes instead, accenting a note here and there in a totally inappropriate fashion that made it even worse for the rest of us. Hongne was the only one to keep a straight face, and his stony disapproval made us apoplectic.

After a week of near onstage disasters, we pulled into a small town in the middle of Normandy not far from Rouen. We were giving a concert as a favor to Lancelot, who was in charge of a small chamber music society there. I didn't think we would get through the evening.

It all started with a furtive glance from Pierlot. I tried desperately not to look at him, but my eyes were drawn to his. I thought Lancelot would drop his clarinet in the middle of the first movement. When Coursier, who looked as if he had absolutely nothing to do with our crazy shenanigans, suddenly let loose with a note more appropriate to a cavalry charge than a quintet, we all had to resort to our handkerchiefs and wipe our eyes. Only Hongne remained immune. And the harsher his glares, the more uncontrollable our tears.

"We can't continue," I said, after the end of the first piece. "We'll have to tell them we've all fallen ill."

"Please, no, we can't do that," pleaded Lancelot. "We'll be all right. Just don't look at anyone else."

"Hmph!" was all we heard from Hongne.

And we launched into the second half of the concert, mortified but still shaking with laughter. I can't imagine what the audience thought of these giggly Parisian musicians, but by evening's end the strain of performing this way had made us extremely tired, edgy and hungry.

"That was a disaster," said Coursier, when we arrived at a nearby restaurant.

"A week-long disaster," added Hongne. "I can't believe you call yourselves professional musicians. Just because we aren't playing in Paris, in front of the critics, doesn't mean we have the right to treat our audiences to a circus performance."

"That's not the point," I said. "An audience is an audience, we all know that. We could just as well have broken up in Paris. I couldn't help it."

I was joined by a chorus of "me neithers," and Hongne harrumphed again. To be honest, we weren't very proud of ourselves, and perhaps all at once realized we absolutely had to stop behaving so stupidly.

"We'll see what happens when we play together next," Lancelot said, "but if this continues, I simply won't be able to take it physically."

Luckily, it didn't. From then on, when our naturally jovial spirits surfaced, they did so *after* the concert. We never again had an evening as bad as that one in Normandy, but I must admit that from time to time I would catch Pierlot's eye to the accompaniment of an oom-pah-pah from Coursier's horn, and the farce was in danger of starting all over again.

The Quintette à Vent was very successful, but less so than another group I brought together later. In 1948 an extremely influential and interesting book by Marc Pincherle had appeared, cataloging the work of Vivaldi in the same way Ludwig von Köchel had cataloged the work of Mozart. I was astonished to find a reference to ten concerti for flute, oboe, bassoon, violin and basso continuo. The original music was in the library of Turin.

At about the same time, the Boîte à Musique company asked me if I would make a Vivaldi recording. The thought of exhuming these manuscripts, which had remained unplayed since the eighteenth century, was very exciting. I ordered the music from Turin and rounded up my friends to see if they would join me in the recording. Pierlot was happy to agree, and so was Paul Hongne. I also asked Robert Veyron-Lacroix and another friend, violinist Robert Gendre, whom I had met on the train we all took to that first postwar music festival in Vichy in 1946. Gendre and I had become fast friends; both of us came from the South of France. He was from Perpignan, and was a proud, fiery Catalan who in his youth had had the great good fortune to study with Luis Pitshot, the violinist friend and partner of the cellist Pablo Casals. As a student, Robert had even played chamber music with Casals.

It would take more than one long-playing disc to record all the Vivaldi, so our group decided to give itself a formal name for the event. I had originally thought we should be called the Ensemble Vivaldi: it suited our purpose, but at the last minute I changed my mind; we had so much fun playing together, and there were so many other composers who wrote music for our special combination of instruments, that it was very likely we would want to enlarge our repertory. Thus was born the Ensemble Baroque de Paris, a chamber music group that lasted for nearly three decades, made numerous recordings and traveled worldwide. We shared the same spirit as the French Wind/Wine Quintet—in fact, the two groups existed simultaneously for several years—and, not surprisingly, Pierlot came up with an equally appropriate nickname: the Ensemble Barrique— the Barrel Ensemble. Fine food, fine wine and fine music always go together in my mind—as, of course, do fine friends.

*

In 1954, I was engaged to play at the Menton Summer Music Festival on the French Riviera. Though by now I spent practically every summer touring the sunspots of Europe, this engagement was special: I was to play a flute and violin recital with Isaac Stern, whose recordings were great favorites of mine, even though I had never met the man himself.

We were both staying at the Menton Palace Hotel, one of those enormous grand edifices that hardly exist any more. After I checked in, I received an urgent message—I was to go to Mr. Stern's room immediately: he wanted to discuss our concert.

Isaac already had an international reputation, and I must admit I was somewhat in awe of him as I rang the bell.

"Come in, come in," was the immediate response. And there, staring at me, was a beaming man wearing nothing but his underpants.

The hair was a little less gray, the body a little less rotund, but the smile was the same one I have come to cherish over the years. From the beginning Isaac was completely natural, and I was impressed by his great warmth.

As we rehearsed our program, I found myself being amazed at the way Isaac played. Listening to him, I discovered a completely different aspect of the music: something I had missed until then. He played— and still plays—in a way that makes each phrase totally personal. It was no longer just notes and phrases, it was beautiful speech, natural and deep—a man telling a story to his son. While this first meeting did not actually change my style of playing, it gave me another dimension through which to approach music.

Isaac and I have remained close friends over the years. We have spent holidays together, and played together around the world. One summer, he, his wife, Vera, and their three children came to stay in Corsica near our home. It was in the early seventies, and though there were all the conveniences necessary for a vacation, there wasn't a phone. To begin with, Isaac assured us this wouldn't bother him, but I wondered how long he'd last, since Isaac is, first and foremost, a phone junkie. He has a phone in every room of his New York apartment, and it seems to me that he has withdrawal symptoms if left without one for more than a few hours. How was he going to survive on the idyllic island of Corsica, with sun, sea, boating, tennis, beaches and plenty of good food, if he didn't have a telephone? There were, in fact, only two phones in our entire village, Sagone, at that time: one at the post office and the other at a small restaurant.

After two days, Isaac asked me about the post office.

"Couldn't we take a trip into town? I'd like to make a call," he said.

"It's not as easy as that," I replied, but agreed to go with him.

The elderly postmistress was sweetness itself.

"Yes, Mr. Stern," she said, "of course you may make a telephone call. What is the number?"

Isaac smiled a smile of triumph, and gave the woman the number. I stood by silently as she picked up the receiver and obviously got through to someone.

"I want to call Paris. The number is—" she began, as Isaac's smile got broader.

The postmistress finished her brief conversation and put down the receiver. She turned toward Isaac. "The call will go through in about an hour and a half," she said. It was my turn to smile.

In the end, when the urge to phone the outside world from paradise got too strong, Isaac took off at midday for the little restaurant in town. He placed his call before ordering his meal, sat down to a hearty lunch and was usually connected with his party by the time he had finished his coffee. It was a relaxing way to indulge in his fetish for communication.

Isaac, thank goodness, has never held it against me that we couldn't provide him with a telephone in Corsica. In fact, we have played together regularly since the "briefs" encounter in Menton. He always inspires me, and I hope I perhaps inspire him, too. There is a kind of osmosis between us, and you can hear it, even on our records. On one occasion, however, things got a little too close for comfort.

It happened back in Menton, at the 1970 Festival, where Isaac and I alternated playing and conducting for each other. At one concert, I led the Mozart G-major Violin Concerto: Isaac was finishing his first-movement cadenza, and we had just come to the tutti where I bring in the orchestra. Most soloists playing a concerto maintain a tremendous rapport with the orchestra, even when they are not actually playing themselves. Maurice André, the great trumpet player, for instance, can hardly restrain himself from conducting along with the conductor. As for myself, I generally turn toward the musicians and just move gently with their beat. Isaac is more exuberant, often playing along with the first violins.

But that night at Menton something went wrong. As Isaac ended his cadenza I turned to my right to bring in the basses and slowly made the semicircular sweep across the orchestra that would bring in the cellos, violas, and then the violins. When I reached them, there was Isaac, practically on top of me. Lost in the music, he had drifted from the left side of the podium. I almost gave my downbeat on his violin. He was so startled that the violin seemed to jump out of its cradle under his chin and hang suspended in midair between us.

This was no ordinary violin, but Isaac's treasured Guarneri, a master's instrument that was virtually irreplaceable and invaluable. For the longest second in his life, Isaac watched the violin sail through the air. I was paralyzed. The orchestra continued to play, but all eyes were on Isaac and the violin.

Isaac leaped to catch it—and did. He held it firmly in his hands, but his impetuous jump brought him down on the podium. All we could do was embrace each other.

Relieved, Isaac finished the concert to thunderous applause; all that was left to do was find sustenance. We had two invitations, and we were obliged to make an appearance at the first, which was at the Princess de Bourbon Parme's magnificent house on the Cap d'Ail. She was a very good friend of mine, and though we were also invited to celebrate Danny Kaye's birthday at the Pirate restaurant just down the road from her villa, I had to at least say good evening to the princess. Isaac and I changed quickly and made our way to Cap d'Ail, where the upper crust of the French Riviera was gathered.

The suppers given by the princess are usually sumptuous, and this was no exception. She is the wife of the Infanta of Spain, King Don Juan's uncle, and she had decided on a traditional Spanish meal: paella. Who can resist such a colorful delicious dish, with its mussels and clams, saffron and tomatoes, peas and sausage? Isaac and I certainly couldn't, so we sat down to eat. Forty-five minutes and two large helpings later, we made our excuses to the princess. The party was wonderful, low-keyed and not too draining, but we said we were tired and had to leave early next morning for Lisbon. We didn't have the nerve to say we'd been invited to another party. By the time we arrived at the Pirate, the fete was in full swing. We seated ourselves on either side of Danny Kaye and Gregory Peck. It was a wild affair, with Danny in the best of spirits. He started mimicking us all: he played the violin like Isaac and the flute like me, and had the whole table in stitches. Of course, Isaac and I couldn't resist sampling the food there as well, and a good deal of the drink, too. The fun lasted

well into the small hours, when eventually the Pirate himself, dressed
in his best pirate's garb, arrived with what we call the *coup de fusil*—
the final shot, the bill. This one rang out so loud I'm sure it was
heard as far away as Marseilles.

Isaac and I stumbled back to our hotel at about 4:00 A.M., fully
aware that we had to be at the airport at seven the next morning.
I went to bed and tried to get a few minutes sleep before packing
my bags, but Isaac's room was directly above mine, and all I could
hear was the steady padding of feet above me, backward and forward,
backward and forward. Isaac was packing. I had forgotten that the
maestro traveled with a minimum of ten suitcases. It would take him
the remaining dawn hours to assemble all his belongings, and I would
be with him every step of the way! We should probably have stuck
with the story we gave the Princess de Bourbon Parme.

Somehow, bleary-eyed and hungover, we made the plane, decidedly
the worse for wear. We were handed the morning paper, and there
was a photo—one the dear princess couldn't help but see—captioned
"A Joyous Quartet" and depicting the far-from-tired faces of Danny
Kaye, Gregory Peck, Isaac Stern and Jean-Pierre Rampal.

*

The 1950s were my formative years as a professional musician. I had
by then completely abandoned all thought of a medical career and
concentrated on my musical schedule. I made friends and contacts
in that decade which have continued to help me throughout my life.

In Paris, my initial exposure to music came through the various
orchestral and chamber music ensembles with which I played. These
included ones that were famous in their day, such as those directed
by Fernand Oubradous and Louis de Froment. Oubradous in particular
influenced my career, and it was through de Froment that I met the
woman who has remained my concert manager to this day: Annie
de Valmalete.

Oubradous's orchestra resembled the Ensemble Baroque on a larger
scale. Oubradous himself was a burly, jovial man with a ready smile
and a great sense of humor. He had had a curious career. It had

started out with the Paris Opera, where he had played the bassoon. Oubradous had, in fact, been *the* bassoonist of his generation. He had hoped to do for the bassoon what Marcel Moyse was doing for the flute, and he researched the repertoire and made numerous recordings that had listeners almost believing that the bassoon could work as a solo instrument. But one day he decided to turn to conducting: he sold his bassoon and never played the instrument again. Oubradous never discussed his change of heart; he simply reiterated that his goal, his great priority, was to create a magnificent chamber orchestra.

Oubradous was very helpful in promoting my career as a soloist. He would schedule flute concerti as part of his Sunday afternoon concerts. The concerts were extremely popular and played a significant part in the musical life of Paris at that time. I performed almost every week, and I'm sure that without the backing and support of Oubradous it would have taken me much longer to make a name for myself.

Even after Obradous laid down his baton, the tradition of the fine chamber ensemble continued. Louis de Froment formed a similar chamber orchestra, using many of the same players, and, of course, imbued with the same spirit. His idea was to assemble the best solo performers in Paris and put together an orchestra that would play and record all the concerti of Mozart. Not surprisingly, the Quintette à Vent was imported lock, stock and barrel for the wind section. Robert Veyron-Lacroix was the soloist in the piano concerti, and Robert Gendre was the concertmaster and soloist for the violin concerti. This "family" stayed together for many years, recording mainly for L'Oiseau-Lyre, owned by our old friend Louise B. M. Dyer, who took a fancy to the strikingly handsome de Froment and his exceptionally fine ensemble. It was with this orchestra that I first recorded Vivaldi's Opus 10, some of my favorite Baroque music that I have since played and rerecorded many times.

When de Froment joined the Luxembourg orchestra as its musical director, his own orchestra dispersed. I continued to play and record with various chamber orchestras throughout France, in particular with two that were directed by Jean-François Paillard and Jean-Pierre

Wallez respectively. Long before de Froment left for Luxembourg, however, he had taken me over to the office of Marcel de Valmalete, Paris's foremost concert producer. The secretary there was Annie de Valmalete, who was following in her father's footsteps.

At that time I did not have a manager; I had put on my Salle Gaveau debut myself, with the help of my wife's grandparents and Gabriel Dussurget. Dussurget's greatest contribution to my career had been to introduce me to Henri Lambert, who had sold me the golden flute; Dussurget had engaged me for a concert or two, and for the Aix-en-Provence Festival one summer, but that had been all. What I needed now was someone who believed in me and in the possibility of a flutist as a soloist.

The Marcel de Valmalete agency was well known in Paris. Segovia was a Valmalete artist, and so were Arthur Rubinstein and Pablo Casals, the violinist Zino Francescati and cellist Pierre Fournier. Valmalete put on recitals in the largest halls in Paris and in the Théâtre de Champs-Elysées and the Salle Gaveau. Marcel himself was a loud man who hid his innate timidity beneath a gruff exterior. He told his daughter Annie to handle me: I would become one of the best-known French artists, he told her. Given that sort of buildup, how could I fail to love the man?

While Marcel occupied himself with the big names, Annie, bright and blonde and ambitious, built up her own stable of younger musicians and composers. She inherited her father's aggressiveness, but she had her own personal rapid-fire way of doing business. Even now, you rarely see Annie without a phone in her hand, another call or two on hold and a pile of contracts on her desk. It took her only a short while to sign up the Quintette à Vent and the Ensemble Baroque, and she signed on Veyron-Lacroix and me as a flute and piano duo. Her sister, Françoise, who also worked for Marcel, signed up Robert Gendre, our violinist, too—to a marriage contract.

Annie worked hard to convince concert and festival managements around France and the rest of the continent that a flute and piano duo could draw a crowd. We played anywhere and everywhere she suggested to help build a following. She pushed me and pushed for me; she shared my hopes and my faith in the flute's future. When we talk about those early years today, Annie plays down the amount of cajoling she had to do, but I know for a fact that if it hadn't been for her tenacity it would have taken me much longer to establish myself as a soloist.

"Of course a flute recital will bring in an audience," I can remember hearing her saying into the phone. "Look at their bios. See how many records they've made. Read the reviews. Jean-Pierre Rampal and Robert Veyron-Lacroix are on the radio all the time. Book them now, and maybe when they're appearing at the Champs-Elysées they'll come back and play for you."

It worked. We had tours and festivals lined up throughout the year. And if the names Rampal and Veyron-Lacroix weren't on everyone's lips immediately, Annie worked hard to make sure they eventually would be. Breaking into the Champs-Elysées crowd was my idea, however.

In France, as in England at that time, the artist had to put on his own recital. There were no sponsors and few managers who would actually pay to arrange concerts. The Théâtre de Champs-Elysées, like the Salle Gaveau, and today the Salle Pleyel, was large, and to arrange an appearance there was an undertaking normally reserved for world-class musicians.

"I'll help you with the organization," said Annie, "but don't you think it's a bit *big*, the Champs-Elysées? That's where the Segovias and the Rubinsteins play."

"I'm sure we can do it," I replied, with the confidence only a thirty-year-old can have, a thirty-year-old who was willing to lay his money on the line to prove his point.

I knew perfectly well that only the most popular artists played the Champs-Elysées. I knew I'd never be like them and play to a sold-out audience the first time. But I did think we could get enough people to cover our costs. Annie started working on the arrangements and Robert and I started rehearsing.

My hubris, my exuberance, paid off—almost. We didn't make any money, but we didn't lose any, either, and in my book that counted as a major success. We decided to do it again, and this time we did make a little money; after that the profits grew along with the audience. I think I helped a whole range of artists who had perhaps been too timid to try for a concert in the Champs-Elysées. Now they knew it could be done successfully by a young performer—and it *was* done, not by a violinist or a cellist, but by a flutist.

"Jean-Pierre, my father was right about you," Annie said, as we settled the accounts for the first concert. "Now we have to see what you can do overseas. Maybe we can even find you a spot as guest soloist with some symphony orchestras."

She was on the phone the very next day. The name Valmalete opened many doors. It's most important to have that kind of professional support when you're breaking new ground, and I believe it was a key to my early success. I didn't become a regular soloist with orchestras immediately, but Annie kept right on pushing. The more records I made, the easier it became, and the more times I sold out the Théâtre de Champs-Elysées the more attention I got.

*

All in all, I look back on the fifties and take a deep breath. Robert Veyron-Lacroix and I made our first international tour—to Indonesia—in 1953 (more about that later) and toured throughout Europe almost every year. I made my United States debut, again with Robert, in 1958, at the Library of Congress, and the next year toured the entire country. And I accepted one of the only steady jobs I've ever had—with the Orchestra of the Paris Opera.

Busy? Yes, I was extraordinarily busy. Playing, traveling, laughing, living. I was young. Whoever thought of easing up in one's thirties? This was my age of discovery.

9

Nights at the Opera and Other Musical Mishaps

BEING A FREELANCE musician is not exactly a steady job. But money was never a real problem, thank goodness, and money has never been all that important to me. I was always able to find enough work to keep my young family quite comfortably.

Françoise and I started out our married life in an apartment attached to her grandparents' house in Neuilly, a leafy suburb west of Paris. We did not live extravagantly, but we always had enough money to go to the movies and out to dinner, and Françoise had a maid to help her with the housework and the children: Isabelle, born in 1948, and Jean-Jacques, who arrived five years later. When Françoise's grandparents died, she and her brother decided to sell the house; we had to start looking for somewhere else to live and began scanning the newspaper advertisements. It was hardly surprising that my eyes were drawn to a boldly printed address on the Avenue Mozart in the 16th arrondissement—it seemed the height of serendipity; I knew the area, of course: it was just a few blocks from Madame Laurens's pension on rue Desbordes-Valmore.

We made two attempts before we succeeded in buying the apartment. The agent who showed us round on our first visit inexplicably played down all the interesting aspects of the place, not even opening the shutters so that we could see it properly. We decided against it almost immediately. Then, two weeks later, we spotted the same advertisement. We decided to give it another try. This time it seemed like a different place entirely, because the agent opened all the shutters, flooding the apartment with the beautiful Parisian sunlight. We bought it on the spot, and have lived there ever since. Appropriately enough, not only is it on the Avenue Mozart, it is just a few yards from a bakery called A la Flûte Enchantée (At the Magic Flute)! The name doesn't have anything to do with me—a *flûte* is a long, skinny loaf of French bread.

Over the years, the apartment has gone through several transformations: at one point Françoise and I rented an identical space three floors above so that my daughter, Isabelle, and her family could live in the apartment we originally bought. Now we have moved back downstairs. The basic character of the place is still unchanged: I have a music room, a separate room in which to store all my records, and there is a warm and cosy living room, decorated in reds and blues and furnished with comfortable period furniture; the vast collection of ornaments lining the walls and corners reflect the huge amount of traveling we've done. A big movie screen descends electronically from the ceiling—a visual counterpoint to the collection of French paintings on the walls. Most of these are nineteenth century, but pride of place is given to the Marc Chagall hanging over the mantelpiece and dedicated to me by the artist.

I am not extravagant but admit I love my comforts. I always travel first class, and have done so from the beginning of my career; I would rather pay a little extra for the flight and maybe scrimp on something else just to ensure that I am not cramped or exhausted when I arrive for a concert.

When I first started performing, I obviously made much less money

than I do now, but I don't recall ever being worried about it. My
mother, however, did enough worrying for both of us. Even though
there were no steady jobs for flute soloists, work was available for
"gentlemen of the orchestra"—orchestral musicians. It was with half
a mind on my mother's worries and the other half on my family—
after all, there were four of us now—that decided me to apply for
a post with the Orchestre de l'Opéra de Paris. I would be able to
continue giving solo performances and still accept touring engagements, but would also have a reliable and regular income.

The Paris Opera Orchestra suited my style of playing. We were
a group of superb musicians, and in those days the Opera Orchestra
was considered one of the finest in Paris. Though all were true
professionals and exceptional musicians, we actually got a lot of fun
out of performing. The atmosphere of the Opera Orchestra was more
relaxed than it is today, and we were nothing if not a large and happy
family, a family that shared a collection of jokes and sometimes
hilarious pranks.

Perhaps some day someone will write about the various minor
dramas that play themselves out in the orchestra pits of the world.
And it will be the members of orchestras who will read them with
the most enjoyment. The pit of Charles Garnier's opera house had
its fair share of pranksters. The little games we played helped to pass
the time, because there were evenings that were definitely less brilliant
than others. One truly great singer would alternate with a far-from-
perfect diva in certain roles, and sitting through four hours of a bad
Bohème twice a week was penance enough for the times when the
music and the singing transcended the stage. We had to find some
way to amuse ourselves.

During the last act of *Aïda*, for example, when the offstage chorus
begins their a cappella melody, it was traditional for the orchestra to
join in. Even our conductor—Georges Sebastian in my day—would
prepare his men: "*Attention, messieurs*, we have our solo. . . ." And he
would give the downbeat with a sweeping gesture. At full force, the
members of the orchestra would add their voices to those of the

Plus ça Change…: Rampal as an infant in Marseilles, circa 1922.

At Your Service: Aged six, in a dapper childhood pose.

Doc Rampal: Before abandoning medical school for music, 1942.

The Perfect Duo: Rampal with his father, Joseph, who at first discouraged Jean-Pierre's flute career.

The Prodigy: By the age of fifteen, Rampal was already distinguishing himself as a musician.

Chantiers de Jeunesse: Rampal playing in the military orchestra.

On the Avenue: With Françoise in Marseilles, 1947.

The Perfect Couple: Rampal married Françoise Bacqueyrisse in 1947.

Five Easy Pieces: Rampal with the talented—and rambunctious—Quintette à Vent Français in the fifties. *From left:* Pierre Pierlot, Gilbert Coursier, Paul Hongne, Rampal, Jacques Lancelot.

Great Gathering: After a Strasbourg Festival concert in 1957. *From left:* cellist Robert Bex, harpist Lily Laskine, alto Colette Lequien, Rampal, composer Francis Poulence and violinist Robert Gendre.

Happy Talk: With violin virtuoso and conductor Sasha Schneider.

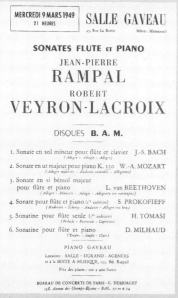

The Great Debut: The program for
Rampal and Robert Veyron-Lacroix's first
Parisian concert in March 1949.

A Dynamic Duo: Rampal with Veyron-
Lacroix. Their musical partnership lasted
for three decades.

Music, Their Love: A meeting
with pianist Arthur Rubinstein,
one of Rampal's idols.

Trio Sonata: Accepting applause
with two of his closest friends,
violinist Isaac Stern (*left*) and
cellist/conductor Slava
Rostropovich.

The French Way: With two other leaders of the Parisian musical world, conductor/pianist Daniel Barenboim (*left*) and composer Pierre Boulez.

All Wrapped Up...: After a performance in Chicago in February 1986, Rampal and accompanist John Steele Ritter sport festive plastic bow ties, part of a yearly joke/gift from friend Elizabeth Stein. (Photo by Elizabeth Stein, courtesy John Steele Ritter)

Tokyo Solo: A TV taping in Japan, where Rampal has become one of the most popular musical stars.

Hamming It Up: Rampal's appearance with Miss Piggy and the Muppets introduced his music to a new audience around the world.

chorus. I myself think it was an improvement, though the chorus was often more than a bit dubious as to our "perfect" pitch.

Another inside joke always occurred in Gounod's *Faust*. A complete ballet was incorporated into the opera, and when the ballerina danced her leading solo, she was accompanied by a musical pas de deux between the bassoonist and a solo cellist in the pit. When the ballerina emerged for her bow, our cellist and bassoonist would also rise, facing each other across the length of the pit. The audience would applaud the dancer, while the orchestra members clapped for their own stars. At least, that was the idea.

Sometimes, the unforeseen happened. Just as I used to get the giggles when playing with my friends from the Quintette à Vin, I was also once stricken with a fit of quite uncontrollable laughter during a performance of Bizet's *Carmen*. It happened at the beginning of the last act, when the alcalde or mayor of Seville arrives to attend the bullfight. His entrance is supposed to be accompanied by two flutes, but Jean-Pierre Eustache, my fellow flutist that evening, was unfamiliar with some of the idiosyncrasies of the Paris Opera's performance. His nervousness was not improved when the two live horses drawing the alcalde's carriage came onstage; they were nervous, too, and began doing—loudly—what horses do when they get anxious. Eustache started laughing helplessly, caught my eye and that was it. First I started, then the oboist and so on, until the entire orchestra was having convulsions. The stunned alcalde had to make a silent entrance. The singers came to the edge of the stage to find out what had gone wrong. Our conductor was kind enough to help us save face: he said we'd had a coughing fit brought on by the dust kicked up by the horses. Tears streaming down our faces, we nodded in agreement.

"Dust from the horses," I murmured. It was as good an explanation as any.

Nights at the opera were by no means all fun and games, however. We did see some tremendous performances, and one of the most memorable was Joan Sutherland's French debut in the 1960 season.

She was singing the title role in Donizetti's *Lucia di Lammermoor*—a virtuoso part for any soprano, and for a flutist, too. The "mad scene" is perhaps one of the finest duets ever written for voice and flute. It was the first time I'd ever heard such a coloratura; it awed me, and I was proud to have accompanied it. Joan scored an enormous triumph that reinforced her position as one of the truly great singers of her generation. When she finished her run of performances in Paris, however, she was replaced by another soprano, one whose voice was weaker in the lower register and stronger in the higher. To accommodate her abilities, she had the cadenza in the "mad scene" transposed from E flat to F. Normally, this is not a difficult transposition— but the conductor, Pierre Dervaux, told us about it only just before raising his baton for the scene. I've always been a good sight-reader, but during that long solo I was looking forward to its close rather than enjoying the challenge it presented.

I played at the Opera every night I was in Paris. But over the years, when my solo engagements required me to travel, I had to cover for myself. I did this with the help of Robert Heriche, a flutist friend of my father who also played in the orchestra. He was my ad hoc impresario and managed to find a replacement for me whenever I was unable to show up. He would pay the flutist who stood in for me, and then I would pay Robert. This all started after my first request for a leave of absence from the Opera was denied. I was about to make my first tour of the United States, which I knew would be vital to my career, but nevertheless the director remained adamant. I was appalled. It wasn't as if I wanted to go and play for the Metropolitan Opera!

The tour contract was already signed, so I decided to go despite being refused permission. Robert Heriche found me a replacement, and I packed my bags and left. When I came back, the director ordered me before a disciplinary committee. I agreed to appear immediately, because I was sure I'd win my case. But the director had just got into trouble with the very same powers he'd wanted to use against *me*—he had been publicly accused of having his hand in the till, and although he'd threatened to sue the newspaper publishing the story, he was, in fact, convicted of fraud. The case of the missing flutist disappeared amid the uproar.

My off-and-on appearances didn't present too many difficulties for the most part, but I do remember being caught in a terrible bind. It was because of Richard Strauss's *Der Rosenkavalier*. I had just returned from a tour and was expecting to play the second flute part in the opera. The second flute is not very difficult, and I'd glanced through the music ahead of time, dutifully practicing the hardest parts. At four o'clock on the day of the performance the phone rang. It was Robert.

"The first flutist is sick, the usual replacement is on vacation and quite unreachable, and you'll have to play first flute tonight," he said, tersely.

I left for the opera house immediately, with barely enough time to shave, found the music and started to read it an hour before curtain time. *Rosenkavalier* is not the easiest of operas, and the first flute part is not the easiest of pieces. I don't think I've ever sweated through a performance like it. If I had thought transposing one aria on the run was difficult, sight-reading an entire score was considerably worse. My eyes barely left the music. Thank heaven, everything went smoothly, and I don't believe the audience ever realized one of the musicians was discovering his part for the very first time.

*

The *Der Rosenkavalier* nightmare was what I like to call one of life's little musical mishaps. When you perform for as long as I have, you're bound to have such unexpected adventures all the time.

Imagine a chamber orchestra onstage and ready to perform. Then someone points out that the first violins don't have their music. This happened at Carnegie Hall in March 1975, when I was the soloist with I Solisti Veneti.

"*Allora!* What are we going to do?" sighed an exasperated Claudio Scimone, the director of the group and a great friend and dining companion of mine.

No one had seen the violinist who was supposed to be in charge of the music. In the backstage rush of black ties and tails, we had just assumed everyone was there. When the orchestra took their seats, however, the gap in the first violins was all too noticeable.

The hour of the concert arrived and passed without the appearance of the stray violinist—and without the appearance of the music. The concert producer, George Schutz, was pacing the wings like a starving lion. Claudio was sweating. The audience, who had braved a fierce ice storm to get to Carnegie, began to rustle, cough, and make all kinds of impatient noises. Ten minutes passed. Fifteen. The unease in the auditorium grew.

"Perhaps he's still at the hotel," someone suggested. Not everyone had flown in on the same plane, and some of the musicians had arrived from Rome just that morning.

Schutz stopped in his tracks and turned to me.

"I don't care what you do; I don't care if you have to play the '1812 Overture' as a flute solo, but get out there and play!" he screamed. "If I have to search every room in that hotel, I will . . ." His voice trailed off as he headed for the exit.

I went onstage and started playing Telemann solo Fantasias. Each time I came to the end of one, I turned to the wings. After the first three or four solos, Claudio just shook his head at me and I launched into yet another.

Meanwhile, Schutz was knocking on every door of the highrise Sheraton Hotel down Seventh Avenue from Carnegie Hall. The violinist was not registered under his own name, which made the search all the more frustrating. He was finally discovered fast asleep, a victim of jet lag. As Schutz snatched up the music and ran, the violinist wearily pulled on his formal clothes and started out for Carnegie. I finished my umpteenth unaccompanied Telemann Fantasia and turned to see, with considerable relief, the broad smiles of Claudio and the exhausted face of Schutz in the wings. No one had a heart attack, and the concert—belatedly—began.

It was I, though, who did most of the suffering one balmy night in Menton on the French Riviera. The concert was being held in a church, and I didn't have a proper dressing room. Waiting to go on,

I sat down on a rather wobbly old chair in the wings, and, unbeknownst to me, a sharp edge on the side of the chair made a small hole in my trousers. As I got up to go onstage, the seam split from top to bottom. There was nothing to be done about it, and no needle and thread handy to repair the damage. If I'd been wearing an ordinary suit, not evening clothes, I could not have performed. My tails covered the split, but I was extremely careful not to bow too low when acknowledging the applause, and when I left the stage I walked as stiffly as a diplomat. No one in the audience suspected a thing.

Such a disaster, though, is far easier to cover up than a laughing fit. As I've said, this is an occupational hazard—especially for me. And when it strikes, there is nothing a flutist can do to produce a sound. A violinist who becomes convulsed with laughter can still bow; a hilarious harpist can still pluck; but a giggling flutist? He has no breath, and his instrument is useless. Though I have suffered this fate with the Quintette à Vent, with Robert Veyron-Lacroix and in the pit at the Paris Opera, the worst of it emerges when I am paired with another flutist. I have never been able to figure out what really starts it off, but once it begins heaven and earth could meet and I'd still have tears streaming down my cheeks.

I remember two particularly embarrassing experiences with Maxence Larrieu and Aurèle Nicolet, both wonderful flutists and very good friends, with whom I had to give up playing at one point because of our predilection for untimely mirth.

Many years ago, Maxence and I were engaged to make a recording of Bach's *St. Matthew Passion* that Erato was producing. We were the only French musicians amid a throng of Germans—a chamber orchestra and two choirs—gathered one day in a small town near Stuttgart. At one point in the music, there is a recitative during which two flutes play a similar melody, one a third above the other.

For some reason, we started to giggle during the first take. Everyone joined in. I suppose they thought these two French flutists were quite hysterical. An hour later, no one was smiling. With each fresh take, our laughing intensified until we were sobbing. The Germans regarded us with steely glares.

"What *is* the matter with you?" hissed Michel Garcin, my musical producer for Erato records. My usually supportive friend had almost had enough of us.

"I can't . . . I can't stop . . ." I sobbed.

The sound engineers changed the microphones so that Maxence and I were back to back. We could keep one eye on the conductor and hopefully get control of ourselves. After several more tries, during which I think the singers were about to beat us up with their scores, we did manage to record a take that Michel Garcin decided to keep. But whenever I listen to that record I can hear the tortured breathing of two convulsed flutists, and I blush to this day. We were mortified.

It was just as bad with Aurèle Nicolet, except that this time it happened onstage during a live performance. Again it was in Germany (perhaps this had something to do with it?) when we were playing a Telemann Trio Sonata for Two Flutes and Continuo. At one point, the first flute begins a richly ornamented passage to which the second flute responds, embellishing the first flute's music; the first flute takes over, with the duet becoming more and more elaborate. It can, in fact, become a vicious spiral, a duel rather than a duet. Nicolet and I had become so involved, and our repartee so complex, that we almost lost control. On that first occasion we managed to escape disaster, but at the next performance of the piece we collapsed as the "duel" began. The laughter took over, and I started shaking so hard that I couldn't go on; I took out my handkerchief and pretended to succumb to an attack of coughing. Nicolet just managed to end his turn, but the tears were streaming down his face. No one guessed we were actually laughing. After all, it was West Germany, and the Germans take their music very seriously.

I add one little aside here for want of a better context. This time, the mistake was a musical one, but not on the part of the musicians. It has to do with a piece written for me by David Diamond, the last movement of which bears a dedication to a certain American music critic.

While touring in the United States in 1986, I happened to give a recital in a town which shall remain nameless in order not to embarrass the critic in question. The recital, with John Steele Ritter, included César Franck's Violin Sonata transcribed for flute, and I thought the performance had gone extremely well.

As it happened, Isaac Stern arrived in the same city later in the day to give a concert himself. He found time to read the review of my concert with considerable glee. He called me immediately.

"Jean-Pierre, Jean-Pierre, just listen to this:" he said, stifling his laughter. " 'Messrs. Rampal and Ritter gave a splendid performance last night, but it was a shame that in the last movement of the Franck Sonata they were unable to keep together.' " With this, Isaac burst into uproarious laughter, and I joined in. The Franck Sonata is best known for the canon in the final movement! If we played it as Monsieur Franck wrote it—as of course we did—there was no way we would have been able to keep together!

I told the story to David Diamond, and when he came to write his Sonata for Flute and Piano, he decided to end the piece with a rousing—and, I might add, ferociously difficult—canon dedicated to the erring reviewer. I appreciated the reference, but in the end John and I were the ones who suffered the most—we had to spend a lot of time practicing that canon so that at the premiere we would sound as if we were running after one another and *not* keeping together.

10

Flirting with Flute Music and Composers

In the years that followed my Salle Gaveau debut, Robert and I traveled throughout France giving recitals. We usually received enthusiastic reviews, which often commented on how strange it was to listen to a whole evening of nothing but flute music and how interesting it was that I played a golden flute! The headline writers had a field day. The critics might have considered our program a novelty at first, but they soon realized the performance was not based on flashy showmanship but on musical integrity.

I have always been extremely serious about my music, and the golden flute was not a gimmick, but a treasure that I loved to play. It linked my present-day playing to the rich heritage of my instrument. Of course, the fact that it helped draw attention to my playing was not such a bad thing either, given that I was breaking new ground. I am proud to say that I have stuck close to my musical roots, never playing music that was cheap or inauthentic. Obviously, some composers are weightier than others. I can, and do, play Mozart and Scott Joplin on the same program and derive as much pleasure from playing the latter as the former; but I recognize the genius of one and the geniality of the other.

Mozart, it is true, is a god for me. Perhaps it is because I find him the most human of composers. If I were stranded on the proverbial desert island and could take only one piece of music with me, I think it would be *Don Giovanni*. If I could take more than one composition, I would pack the entire works of Mozart. But also I would be very frustrated to be unable to bring some scores of Bach, Brahms, Schubert, Beethoven, Debussy, Ravel and more, and more!! . . . (That is always the crucial problem when people ask you what one piece of music you would take to a desert island.)

It is not always useful to analyze just why a composer is important: one should just feel it. Mozart encompasses a range of feelings that are profoundly satisfying to me. His music is full of charm and spirit, sadness and great emotion—and, of course, great humor, all of which proves how well he understood the human spirit. This comes across very clearly in his letters, where one sees his mood change from day to day, sees his joy lightening his whole world or his despair weakening his resolve. We see the Mozart the movie *Amadeus* brought to life so beautifully: a fun-loving trickster, a scatological humorist, a wild child, a hard-working composer. Mozart earned a fair amount of money in his life, but whenever he found himself in funds he always spent every penny, providing lavish entertainment for his friends. His goal always appears to have been to please others, and he had the truly human need for approbation, too. He is a mixture of triviality and *grande noblesse*—a child masquerading as a composer. The paradox, of course, is that such a human being could produce such sublime music. But I do not question the origin of genius.

What I do question, and must admit am frequently quite annoyed by, are the usual program notes about the Mozart flute concerti. Invariably some dull-minded musicologist will regurgitate the phrase: "Everyone knows that Mozart hated the flute. . . ." This is just a little too simple an interpretation of a couple of lines from a letter

Mozart wrote to his father early in 1778, when he was struggling to finish a commission for De Jean, or, more exactly, De Jong, a Dutch amateur flutist. Mozart's good friend Johann Wendling, a great German flutist of the day, had introduced Mozart to De Jean, who was his pupil. De Jean, who was quite wealthy, commissioned several works from Mozart, including a flute concerto and three quartets.

Mozart always took pride in what he wrote. If he signed a work, it was because he felt it was worthy of being left to posterity: he had an innate sense of how the future would judge his compositions. Despite the fact that he was behind schedule with the commissioned quartets, he finished the flute concerto and delivered it to De Jean, fully expecting to be paid for it. At that time he was struggling, as well, with a very complicated love life: one woman had rejected his advances, and he had just become enamored of another, an opera singer named Aloysia Weber. She, however, was none too sure of her feelings about the composer, and he finally married her sister, Constanze.

On February 14, 1778, Mozart's exasperation was apparent in the letter he wrote to his father. He complained that De Jean had never paid him for the flute concerto and that he didn't know how he would be able to write down all the pieces floating around in his head, what with having to complete the rest of the Dutchman's commissions. It is here that the misleading line "I must write incessantly for an *instrument* that I cannot stand" appears. The *instrument* is, of course, De Jean, not the flute itself.

This was an age of amateurs, and scores of people were trying their hand at the flute; the time was rife with flutemania, and this might have added to Mozart's exasperation. Nonetheless, his orchestral and operatic work includes many important and beautiful flute parts, in addition to the two concerti, and this proves to me that he simply could not have *hated* the instrument. The G-major Concerto turned out to be too serious and too difficult for De Jean, who had specifically commissioned a light, easy piece. Mozart retrieved it and gave De Jean a concerto in D major instead. This was a transcription of his work for oboe written the previous year. He transposed the key from C to D and augmented the solo part. The D-major Concerto is simpler than the G-major, and at one time was more popular because the orchestral accompaniment is also easier. De Jean never finished paying Mozart.

I cannot be convinced that Mozart disliked the flute. As was often the case with him, he was probably simply having a temper tantrum. Had he been asked, a week later, if he meant what he had written, he would have replied incredulously, "What do you mean, I called the flute a detestable instrument?" Because Mozart is a god to me and because I am a flutist, I find it impossible to believe in a god who didn't like the flute.

One cannot play God's music all the time, but no matter who composed the music, I must love it while I am playing it. It is that rapport with the music that brings it alive for an audience. Whether the piece is by Mozart or even Salieri (a composer for whom I share Mozart's disdain), I must feel real affection for it. Whenever you play music, you have to believe in it or the audience will not accept it.

Playing so-called marginal composers is not a way to fill a program or increase one's repertoire. Neither is transcribing music written for another instrument. The flute repertoire itself, contrary to many beliefs, is extremely rich and varied, even though it does not carry the weight of the repertoire for the violin or piano. And the nineteenth-century composers did not do their best by it.

Transcribing has always been a controversial subject. People sometimes claim that it is dishonest to play music on one instrument that was specifically written for another. I play transcriptions of eighteenth-century chamber music because it was written for a variety of instruments of the day; the parts were rarely composed with a specific instrument in mind. In those days, people played chamber music at home in much the same way we play stereos or watch television today, picking up whatever instrument they happened to have around and knew how to play. Composers of that time wouldn't have been in the least disturbed that a part written for the flute would be played by the violin in one house, or vice versa; they wanted their music *played*, and considered the violin and the flute interchangeable. So did the performers.

I have transcribed concerti and sonatas, but only when specifically asked to by the composer, for teaching purposes, or when the original instrument no longer exists, as is the case with the A-minor Arpeggione Sonata by Schubert.

The arpeggione was a stringed instrument somewhere between a guitar and a viola or small cello. It had six strings that were tuned like those of a guitar, but it was played with a bow. Although this description may sound promising, the sound it produced was far from exciting. It was first introduced in Vienna in 1823, the creation of a Herr Stauffer, who obviously hoped that it would be widely played. Stauffer even commissioned Schubert to write a piece to promote the instrument. This hybrid monstrosity died in less than ten years, and there can't be more than a couple of dozen in existence. The Schubert sonata still survives, however.

The music was written in a key that works as well for the flute as for a stringed instrument, so why not play it on the flute? Most cellists and viola players take the piece as written for them, because the small cello or viola are probably the closest instruments to the arpeggione available to us today. But there is no reason to think that one betrays the music by playing it on the flute, and I am sure that Schubert would have been more than pleased to hear anyone *but* an arpeggionist play his beautiful sonata.

There are transcriptions and transcriptions, however. Some are impossible because they destroy the spirit and sense of the music, while some can be made without hurting the original. When playing compositions that were not originally written for the flute, I always ask myself if the transcription lessens the composer's intent.

It never occurred to me, even in a weak moment, to try and play the Brahms Violin Concerto on the flute. It would betray the thought and inspiration of the composer completely: it would be a gratuitous circus turn. The same goes for Beethoven's Violin Concerto. William Bennett, the wonderful English flautist and a good friend of mine, did make a recording of the piece as transcribed for the flute, but although it is well done, I must admit I find it shocking. The work is just too famous on the violin to go over well on the flute. However, Beethoven himself, probably for base financial reasons—wrote a horrible version of that same piece for the piano. This proves to me that composers are much less sensitive to the idea of transcriptions of their works than are some narrow-minded musicologists, who—as we say in France—are often more royalist than the king himself!

My brief flirtations with violin concerti have been wholly honorable.

Aram Khachaturian asked me to transcribe his Violin Concerto for the flute, and I was only too happy to do so. I first met Khachaturian in Prague about twenty-five years ago when I was premiering a flute concerto by Jindřich Feld, a young Czech composer, with the Czech Philharmonic. The Feld Concerto is quite unlike most contemporary flute concerti: it is sweeping, romantic, intense and darkly brooding, with a kind of dramaticism rarely encountered in flute music. I think the power of the piece impressed Khachaturian and Dmitri Shostakovich, who happened to be in Prague at the same time and also attended the concert.

I was introduced to Shostakovich. Unfortunately, we shared no common language and had no adequate translators. In any event, I attempted to ask him if he would consider writing a flute concerto. The language barrier and my inherent shyness in front of the great man rendered my request barely intelligible, and the only answer I got from him was a warm "Why not?" But I visited Russia so rarely that I was unable to establish a rapport with him, and the concerto was never written.

I was lunching with friends in Prague that same week, and Khachaturian was there, too. He was a bearlike Armenian with an immense love of life that emerges clearly in his music. I asked him if he'd ever been inspired to compose music for the flute.

"After hearing you play the Feld Concerto, I recognize that it's possible for the flute to play a long, dramatic piece," he said. "Why don't you take my Violin Concerto and see if a transcription of it would work for you?"

I took him only half seriously, wondering if the gesture was simply the result of a fine and mellowing lunch. I did not know his Violin Concerto at all well.

"I'd love to see if it's possible," I replied, thinking he'd probably made the suggestion just to get rid of me.

Back in Paris, I bought the score of the Khachaturian Violin Concerto, and set about transcribing it. At once it was apparent that it would be possible to do this while still keeping the dramatic quality of the original. Very few double stops occur in the melodic line— chords where you have to play two notes at the same time. This is routine on the violin, but impossible on a flute. (The Brahms Violin Concerto, by contrast, has many double stops.)

When I had finished the transcription, I sent it to Khachaturian, suggesting that, in order to give the work authenticity as a flute concerto, he should write new cadenzas. We met again in Paris shortly afterward, and he threw up his hands in horror at my request.

"Jean-Pierre, I'll give you permission to publish the work," he said, "but as for the cadenza, you must write it yourself. When I originally wrote the concerto for David Oistrakh, I wrote a cadenza into it myself. David didn't like it and wrote one for himself. My work had been a complete waste of time, and I'm not going to have the same thing happen all over again!"

The transcription of the Khachaturian Concerto was eventually published—with my own cadenzas. Today it is one of the most popular of flute pieces, recorded and played by scores of flute soloists.

*

I have been very fortunate during my career to work closely with composers as well as with fellow musicians. This forms an important part of the process of developing an environment in which the flute will be noticed and composed for. The Baroque repertoire, of course, is rich and varied, but, by contrast, that of the nineteenth century is something of a wasteland. Twentieth-century composers, however, have paid more attention to the instrument, giving flutists some uncut gems which we can polish for public performance.

For me, working with a composer is like working with a link to the past. Composers follow in the traditions that gave us Bach and Mozart, Beethoven and Brahms. They move music forward, and though I am no fan of twelve-tone music, in the fifties I did play it quite often. In fact, I recorded one of the first versions of Arnold Schoenberg's *Pierrot Lunaire* and performed many pieces by such avant-garde composers as René Leibowitz. My chance to play a work by Pierre Boulez, however, came and went—which was unfortunate, because I rather liked it.

Boulez wanted to write a piece for the flute, and I was honored to be asked to play it. I had met Boulez at the Paris Conservatory. He was very tough-minded, passionate and intellectual. He didn't like much of anything in music: he was against Beethoven, against Mozart, against Ravel—though he did like Bach. He has changed since, of course, and has even conducted a concert in which I played a Mozart flute concerto, and made a recording with me of the C. P. E. Bach D-minor Concerto. When I first met him, though, he was in his rebellious period, and very little pleased him.

He wrote his Sonatina for Flute and Piano and sent me my part. He wanted me to play the work with a favorite pianist of his rather than with my partner, Robert Veyron-Lacroix, because he didn't think Robert's style was right for the music. For his part, Robert wasn't all that keen on Boulez's music, either.

As far as notation was concerned, the music was extremely difficult to decipher—and I'm a good sight-reader. There were no measure bars or any other helpful signs. I could sense that the work had a strong emotional appeal, but with an extremely heavy concert sched-ule, the idea of spending hours, perhaps even days, picking my way through a difficult modern work was sapping my spirit.

Cautiously I asked if he could put in a few measure bars.

"Play it as it's written. The unity of the rhythm is counted at the beat," he replied, ever true to his principles.

But without measure bars, the rests are difficult to follow and it is really a nuisance to play. I sent the music back, and again asked Boulez if he could make me a cleaner—and clearer—copy.

Perhaps this upset him, because time passed and I heard nothing further. I must admit that the piece slipped my mind, too. I'm glad he finally produced a clean copy and found a flutist to play it, because it is a striking, energetic work that moves along with the speed of a cardiograph gone wild. I am sorry I've never performed it. I still have the score, bearing a dedication to me, and I still consider Boulez a friend, as well as one of the greatest, perhaps *the* greatest, musical genius of this century.

I understand the force that makes people determined to come up with new compositional ideas, and have nothing against such music itself. However, I prefer music that *sings*, music the soul can enter into. The Boulez Sonatina is ultramodern in style, but it resonates with an emotionalism one cannot ignore. Had Boulez showed it to me in the form in which it was eventually published, I would have made more of an effort to learn it. I play some pieces by André Jolivet that in their time were considered excessively modern, and which performers such as Moyse refused to touch because they thought them too advanced. But I heard them differently: I heard the song within them. I do not play music that I do not feel in my heart.

*

I worked with André Jolivet and Francis Poulenc in Paris in the fifties. Out of these relationships have sprung some beautiful flute pieces. One of these is a Poulenc Flute and Piano Sonata that helped my career in the United States (and of which I shall say more later).

I once suggested to Jolivet that he might do well to write a piece for flute and percussion. He had always leaned toward tribal and earthy sounds in his music, and I felt he would do justice to the contrast such instruments would provide. He came up with an extraordinary work for flute and "dry" percussion—percussion without pitch: it includes drums but not xylophones, for example. I had the honor of premiering this in Paris.

Working with Jolivet was always interesting. He had quite fixed ideas as to how his music should sound, but at the same time he let his musicians voice their own opinions. He wanted to give his soloist free rein to suggest things that were more appropriate for his or her instrument, but at the same time he knew exactly what he wanted the overall spirit of the work to be, down to the smallest details.

Jolivet himself conducted both the premiere and the recording of his work. The slow movement is very regal, very somber, even funereal, and I suggested to Jolivet that I play it on an alto flute, which has a darker, lower pitch. He was not at first convinced that this would work, but I asked him to let me try it at least once. There were no transposition problems, because dry percussion has no tonality, and I was able to transpose the flute line as I played. When Jolivet heard the piece performed this way, he was immediately won over. "Ah, it's exactly right," he said. "It's as if the sound comes from the Valley of the Kings, from the depths of the earth."

*

Florent Schmitt, who was born in 1870, was already an old man renowned for his choral compositions and ballet scores when I first met him in Paris in the fifties. He was very small, with a dry manner. As a young man he had been a pianist, but as his eyesight dimmed with age, so did his playing. He lived in Saint Cloud, across the Seine from Paris, and I had often been at his house for the *jeudis de Florent Schmitt*, as his Thursday-afternoon gatherings were called. The whole of Paris's musical world could be found there at one time or another. I am still thrilled today when I remember some of the conversations we used to have. We spoke of Ravel and Saint-Saëns, and there were always older people there who would say things like, "Ah, yes, Saint-Saëns! I knew him well. We were such great friends!"

It was a tangible link with the past.

I particularly remember two venerable composers who attended these salons regularly: Gustave Samazeuilh and Henri Busser.

Samazeuilh had been a great friend of Debussy's; he typified the cultured European gentleman, polite, well read and with an extraordinary memory. He adored cornering some unsuspecting youngster at M. Schmitt's and regaling him with tales of the past. Schmitt, who was good at making up clever nicknames, called Samazeuilh *l'Insistance Publique*, a pun on *l'Assistance Publique*—the French for public assistance or what in the States would be called welfare. When he started to talk it was almost impossible to escape. Still, one was never bored when captured by Samazeuilh; I could—and did—listen to his tales many times over. He talked of people I revered as old masters as if he had just left their drawing rooms. You would think that Debussy was still living to hear Gustave speak. His memories went even further back: he used to tell us of the day when, as a very young boy, his parents had taken him to a house where he saw Liszt sitting in the parlor playing the piano. The great composer had picked him up and sat him on his lap. It was incredible to me to meet someone who had actually met Liszt. The story had an apocryphal ring to it, but what did that matter?

Henri Busser told an even taller tale of Brahms. Busser, who was one of Massenet's students, was refused admittance to Brahms's house. He and a companion had set out to visit *le maître* in Germany, reaching their destination only after a long and arduous journey. They found the Brahms residence and rang the doorbell. A butler answered the door, and, in the background, the young men caught a glimpse of a bulky back and a head of long gray hair. The butler asked their business.

"We are two French composers come to see *le maître*," they answered.

"Wait one moment," said the butler.

He turned to convey the information to his employer. The young men heard a grunt and then the words, "French composers? Huh, they're all *merde*."

The butler closed the door in their faces, and, disappointed and somewhat shocked at being referred to as shit, the two left.

Can you imagine talking to someone who had been—or claimed to have been—that close to Brahms? It was as thrilling as playing concerts in halls that echoed with the great names of the past. My second major recital with Robert Veyron-Lacroix was held in the old Paris Conservatory concert hall, a room where Chopin and Liszt were once regular attractions. Unfortunately, despite the fact that it is one of the best halls acoustically, the room holds only about seven or eight hundred people, and it is no longer used for concerts.

Once while playing in Vienna, Denis Evesque, the French cultural attaché and a fine pianist, took me to visit the palace of Prince Lobkowitz, one of Beethoven's patrons. It was here, in a small room that could hold barely a hundred people and with a stage capable of accommodating an orchestra of no more than twenty-five, that Beethoven had given the first performance of his Third Symphony, the *Eroica*, in 1804. The musicians who performed that night signed, as was the custom in those days, receipts acknowledging that they'd been paid for their work. These receipts can still be seen in the palace archives. They somehow bring that long-ago performance very much to life.

The room, which is now called the "Eroica" room, has hardly changed since then. For all I could tell, the chairs were the same ones that were used on that famous occasion. I was enchanted and moved. Denis and I often played together, and when he suggested that we organize a small soirée to be held in the Salle Eroica, I didn't hesitate. It was with something of a beating heart that I took the same stage in the same room and with perhaps the same furnishings that Beethoven had occupied.

I have always sensed links to the past very strongly, and because of this tried to attend as many of Florent Schmitt's *jeudis* as possible. One afternoon I asked him if he was interested in writing a flute concerto. He wasn't what you'd call an avant-garde composer, being more closely allied to the style of the past—the style of Ravel, for example, who was his contemporary. He was less modern than Jolivet or Boulez, but he was as modern as Poulenc, and he had a fine reputation. I always believed, not only for my own benefit but for the benefit of future flutists, that it was my duty to try to develop the repertoire as much as possible.

I always regretted that the previous generation of great flutists did not push the composers of their time to write concerti or sonatas for the flute. If I had been a violinist, I would have done the same thing for the violin. The flute is my own personal way of expressing music. But you have to think not only of your own career but of what will happen after you are gone. My campaign to encourage contemporary composers to write for the flute is based on this philosophy. I have always thought it a tremendous loss that Ravel, for example, never composed a flute concerto: he composed so well for the instrument. His Introduction and Allegro for Harp, Flute, Clarinet and String Quartet is a beautiful work that shows how well he understood the flute. If only a great flutist of that time had asked and kept on asking him, he would have written a flute solo that would have been a masterpiece. I am sure of it.

Once when I played in Washington, D.C., with the National Symphony Orchestra, Rostropovich was conducting a symphony by Ezra Laderman for full orchestra on the same program. I heard the piece three or four times during my engagement and each time was impressed by the scale and scope of the music. It occurred to me that Laderman might well be interested in tackling a concerto for flute and large orchestra. He was in Washington at the time, and we discussed the project. When he received a commision from the Detroit Symphony, he decided to pursue the idea seriously.

In the course of writing the piece, he sent me sketches of part of the music to see if they were appropriate for the flute; I was able to work very closely with him. The Concerto places the flute in the center of the orchestra, where it holds its own. The work is nearly half an hour long, rare for flute music these days, and has the dimensions of a large orchestral work. "Dramatic" and "meaty" would be good words to describe it, and when I had the honor of premiering the work in Detroit—and at New York's Carnegie Hall—it met with wonderful acclaim.

Another suggestion that worked out well involved Leonard Bernstein. In 1981 he wrote a piece for flute and orchestra—*Halil* (which means "flute" in Hebrew)—that we premiered in Israel on the occasion of the fiftieth birthday celebrations of Teddy Kollek, the mayor of Israel. Lenny is a veritable *force de nature*, as is the work itself, a swirling celebratory piece that was fun both to learn and perform.

Working with Lenny was also a whirlwind experience. After rehearsing all day, playing all evening and celebrating all night, he still wanted to party until dawn. I don't think he ever sleeps. On one occasion I went along with him until three in the morning and then I gave up.

"Jean-Pierre, you've got to come with me!" he said, as we left yet another restaurant.

"I've just got to get some sleep. I don't know about you, but I'm dead," I protested wearily. "*Bonne nuit, bon courage et bonne chance!*"

*

Florent Schmitt was not very well known internationally, but I felt convinced that he could, and should, write something for the flute. We corresponded about the project, and one day I received a letter asking me to come to his Saint Cloud apartment to go over the music.

"*Voilà!* My concerto, which I call 'Suite for Flute and Orchestra,' " he said when I arrived. Then he suggested we play it through together.

I stood behind him as he sat at the piano and tried to read over his shoulder. Even though his nose was just about touching the score, he wasn't having much luck. And he was blocking my view almost entirely. He played an approximation of the tightly written score, and I played what I could see of the extremely complicated music. We must have presented a very funny picture: a tall flutist bending over a small gray man squinting at an almost illegible score.

"That's very good," he said at the end, "very good."

I wasn't quite so convinced. I had barely been able to see the music, let alone play it.

"*Maître*, could I please keep the music so that I can work on it?" I asked, rather embarrassed at my performance.

"You played very well, very well," Schmitt reiterated, keeping a firm hold on the music.

"But I was just sight-reading, and the flute part is written so small I can hardly tell if it's playable," I protested.

"I think you played very well, but I'll make you a copy if you wish," he answered.

Several weeks later the music arrived. I had my copy—but the music had already been published! There wasn't a chance of changing a single note, and some of it was excruciatingly difficult. Nevertheless, I agreed to give the premiere with the Orchestre National. I had to be on tour prior to the concert, but spent all my evenings working on the new music.

I arrived in Paris three days before the event and expected to go into immediate rehearsal. My manager called me at home.

"The concert with the Orchestre National is canceled."

"Why? What's happened?"

"They couldn't locate the orchestra score. Mr. Schmitt is accusing the publisher of having lost it, and it was his only copy. He's absolutely livid, and he's threatening to sue."

"Well, we'll just have to reschedule the concert when they come up with the music," I said.

I never did get to play the Schmitt concerto. The music never turned up. Many years passed, and just before Schmitt's death it was discovered that he had forgotten to orchestrate the piece, and then forgotten that he'd forgotten. Only the flute and piano parts exist today.

11

Thank You, Elizabeth Coolidge, Thank You!

EVEN IN THE FIFTIES, with my career progressing steadily in Europe, I knew that my next real challenge was the United States. America fascinated me, not least because of its tremendous size. So even while I was starting to play in major concert halls in London, Paris and Berlin, my sights were set on the New World. My records were already on sale there, but I had no idea of what sort of reception I'd get in person. Would Americans want to listen to a French flutist? Robert Veyron-Lacroix and I took off to find out.

If there's anyone to thank for giving me the opportunity, it's Elizabeth Sprague Coolidge, or, perhaps more accurately, the Elizabeth Sprague Coolidge Foundation at the Library of Congress in Washington, which arranged my debut. And the story all started with a phone call in 1957 from Francis Poulenc.

"Jean-Pierre, you know you've always wanted me to write a sonata for flute and piano? Well, I'm going to," he said. "And the best thing is that the Americans will pay for it! I've been commissioned by the Coolidge Foundation to write a chamber piece in memory of Elizabeth Coolidge. *I* never knew her, so I think the piece is yours."

"That sounds wonderful," I replied, "but will they accept a piano and flute sonata, instead of a chamber work?"

"I just don't think I can write a piece of chamber music. I wrote a very bad string trio, and I tried to do a string quartet, but it's even worse—it's still unfinished. I really only succeed when I'm writing for two distinct voices."

It's perfectly true. Poulenc's Sextet for Wind Quintet (which makes up one of the voices) plus piano is wonderful, as, of course, is his vocal work. And later he used to say of his Flute and Piano Sonata, "Just imagine what would happen if I transcribed it for flute and *orchestra*! It would be absolutely dreadful!"

He was right again. Lennox Berkeley, a fairly prolific English composer with—normally—a very fine musical intelligence, did actually orchestrate this Sonata. It was just as well Poulenc never lived to hear it, because I'm sure he'd have put his hands over his ears in horror. I was once asked to play the piece with the added orchestral accompaniment and firmly refused to do so. "Absolutely not," I said. "It's *vulgar*!"

A month or so after we'd talked about the Sonata, Francis phoned again. He was in mid-rehearsal for his extraordinary *Dialogues des Carmelites* at the Paris Opera, but he said he'd finished a version of the Flute Sonata and would like me to come and play it with him.

Francis lived in a top-floor apartment overlooking the Jardins du Luxembourg, near the little square which today bears his name. His place was small but comfortable, a grand piano dominating the living room. His angular frame was similarly imposing, and though you couldn't call him handsome—his features were all larger than life, especially his ears—he had a forceful charm that was quite winning when he was not suffering from the depressions that would so often haunt him.

When I arrived, he handed me the music—or, rather, a scrap of music.

"We will play it together," he said. "It will be very good."

I was not so sure. The first movement seemed disjointed, and there wasn't much of a theme or direction. The ideas came and went, but had no real coherence. And some of the fingering was impossible. I said so.

"This is how I work," he replied. "You will see. It will be very good."

Not long afterward, he called me again and asked if I'd come over and try some of the revisions he'd done. When I got there, I saw that his ideas were more coherent this time, but still far from finished.

"You take this," he said when we were through, handing me the music. "See if it's playable."

So off I went with a collection of bits and pieces that didn't resemble a flute sonata at all. We worked this way for several months, with me periodically showing up at his apartment, trying out whatever he'd written and then taking it away with me. I did change a few phrases here and there and gave Francis some ideas as to how the work should hang together, but I must admit that at the beginning I was rather panicky. I simply couldn't see where the piece was going—and was very much afraid Francis couldn't, either. Yet he became more confident, and slowly but surely the Sonata for Flute and Piano took its final shape.

In January 1958, the Coolidge Foundation gave Poulenc permission to perform the piece, with me playing the flute part, at the Strasbourg Festival. The Washington, D.C., debut was set for Valentine's Day. I arrived in Strasbourg two days before the concert in order to have plenty of time to practice with Francis. Poulenc was not noted for his punctuality at rehearsals, and sometimes hadn't even learned his part by the time the concert was supposed to begin. I once asked him—we were making a recording at the time—if he'd studied his part. "Not much," he said, "but when I come to the bits I don't know, I can always keep my foot on the pedal." (Unfortunately this is an option a flutist doesn't have. Many's the time I'd have liked to have a pedal I could hold down in order to see my way through a bar that was mastering *me*!)

On the morning before the first performance, Poulenc called me. "Arthur Rubinstein is here," he said. "I've just talked to him, and he very much wants to hear my new sonata. The only trouble is, he has to leave tomorrow before the performance. Do you think you could come over right now and have just one more rehearsal?"

"With pleasure," I replied.

So the unofficial premiere of the Poulenc Sonata for Flute and Piano took place in a concert hall in Strasbourg with an audience of one—Arthur Rubinstein, sitting in the middle of the front row. The applause we received from him was as memorable as at any concert I have played. Twenty years later, when we ran into each other in the Drake Hotel in New York, the first thing Arthur said to me was, "Do you remember the premiere of Francis's Flute Sonata in 1958, during the Strasbourg Festival?" (The reputation of Rubinstein's fantastic memory is not false!)

How could I ever forget? Rubinstein's enthusiastic response meant a very great deal to me, and the Sonata itself was responsible for launching my career in the United States. It will always hold a special place in my memory. When the first edition was published, I was credited with editing the flute part—but unfortunately my name was misspelled. So much for posterity. . . .

Anyway, after a successful performance in Strasbourg—before a huge audience, this time—I rejoined Robert Veyron-Lacroix for the start of our American tour. We were scheduled to visit Mexico, drop into Washington, D.C., for the day, where Francis and I were scheduled to play the Sonata during a program of Poulenc's work, then head north for engagements in Montreal and Toronto.

But in Mexico City, I received an urgent call from Francis. He wanted to know if Robert could take his place at the Library of Congress concert. Since he had no other reason to come to the States, he didn't want to make the long journey for just one evening. The Coolidge Foundation, he told me, was prepared to change the program, if Robert and I agreed. Of course, we said.

So instead of my debut in the United States being part of a tribute to Poulenc, the concert became a flute and piano recital in which the Poulenc Sonata would simply be one number, albeit an important one.

Along with the Poulenc, we performed Handel, Bach and Prokofiev; and, if I do say so myself, things went exceedingly well. Fortunately, the critics thought so, too. The next day we opened the newspapers to utter delight. Day Thorpe in the *Evening Star* wrote: "Although I have heard many great flute players, the magic of Rampal still seems to be unique. In his hands, the flute is three or four music makers— dark and ominous, bright and pastoral, gay and salty, amorous and limpid. The virtuosity of the technique in rapid passages simply cannot be indicated in words." And Paul Hume in the *Washington Post* commented: "They gave a program which increased in brilliance as the evening progressed." I couldn't have written better reviews myself.

The champagne was on ice and congratulations resounded. More important than anything, however, was the request by a young concert promoter to sign us up for a tour that very year. The pioneering Rampal and Veyron-Lacroix duo were about to take on America.

*

Only the wildest of imaginations could say we took the country by storm. We did tour extensively, hoping to build up a reputation, but unfortunately our first concert organizer was better at booking dates than at geography.

Her name was Janet Loren, and she was enterprising, young and energetic—but poorly schooled in the layout of her country. She decided to take a risk in promoting us and managed to arrange concerts in at least twenty different towns on that first swing through the States. However, her bizarre schedule kept us flying and driving halfway across the continent and back every few days. We did get good audiences—all the halls, for the most part community centers and college campuses, were full—but in some of those remote towns in the middle of nowhere we two Frenchmen, with our Gallic "command" of English, found ourselves decidedly out of place. Especially when we had to play to the accompaniment of clattering knives and forks.

One night we drove all over a small Florida town looking for the community auditorium. It felt as if we'd been on the road for days. Planes had brought us within a few hundred miles of our destination, but we had had to drive the rest of the way. And when we arrived, the audience had just started dinner.

Now an ideal audience is attentive and undistracted. The music should be appreciated, perhaps in the same way and spirit as a fine dinner, but not at the same time. Janet had managed to book us into some dinner-theater locales. Neither Robert nor I appreciated performing in places better suited to *Hello, Dolly!* On this particular occasion, we made our way to the piano, set up our music and prepared for battle. But what is one flute and one piano against an orchestra of silverware? We easily lost the first round to the prime ribs. From there on, we played as fast as we could, leaving out the repeats, hating every moment of playing to an audience that had its collective mouth full.

Perhaps the dessert was less interesting than the beef, because when we finished our program, there was a thunderous reception. We would have to play an encore. I wasn't sure who started laughing first, but by the time we were midway through Debussy's "Little Shepherd" from his *Children's Corner* Suite, Robert and I were practically crying. He was doubled up on the piano stool and I had to fake a coughing fit to wipe the tears from my eyes. Maybe it was the array of loud sports coats and white patent-leather shoes, or the mere absurdity of our situation: Had we really flown and driven a thousand miles to play Mozart for people picking strawberry seeds out of their false teeth?

Our audience remained loyal and clapped so hard we knew we had to give a second encore. This time we really did have to give up halfway through, but I don't think anyone noticed. We left the hall just as coffee was being served.

I think we spent more money that first year on air fare than we made in concert fees. The halls, big, small and middle-sized, were always crowded, but we couldn't stick to such an exhausting schedule.

Traveling from sea to shining sea was wonderful, but not three times a week. Something had to be done.

The break came at a party. Julius Baker, first flutist of the New York Philharmonic, introduced me to a young lady who worked for a New York artists' management company. After I started complaining bitterly about my touring schedule, she suggested I come and see her employers, Henry and Ann Colbert.

I did so the very next week. Even the location of Colbert Artists was auspicious—on West Fifty-seventh Street, right across from Carnegie Hall. For me, Carnegie has always been the most inspiring of concert halls: it echoes with reputations made, masterworks premiered—the sense of linking the old with the new, of the continuity of great music. As Robert and I made our way to the Colberts, I hoped with all my heart, one day, to be on the other side of the street, preparing for my Carnegie Hall debut.

Ann Colbert was very optimistic about our chances in the States, because many of our recordings had become well known there. Her enthusiasm was heartening—after all, Colbert Artists managed some of the biggest names of the day, and, like Marcel de Valmalete in Paris, was able to arrange for bookings at all the major concert halls. A flutist and a pianist might not be ready for Carnegie Hall immediately, but with the help of Colbert Artists, and Agnes Eisenberger, who became our personal manager there, we would be able to make sense of our travel plans and start building a new career.

"The college dates are very important," said Agnes, a petite but forceful woman cast in the same mold as Annie de Valmalete. "We start out with colleges first, then we can slowly work our way back toward New York . . . and Carnegie Hall."

"May we *please* avoid dinner recitals?" I begged. "I love to eat and I love to play music, but I don't like people doing something I love to do while I'm forced to do the other. They don't appreciate the music, and anyway it makes me hungry."

"Angry?" asked Agnes. My French accent was pretty strong in those days.

"No, *hungry. We* never eat before a concert; why must we watch everyone else fill their stomachs while we go hungry?"

"Oh, I'm fairly sure we can avoid those dinner recitals next time," Agnes said with a smile. And we did.

Robert and I added America to our yearly travel plans. I couldn't begin to list everywhere we played, always before an exemplary public. Unlike Europe, America is not caught up in the kind of snobbism and traditionalism that can so readily stifle a musician's enthusiasm. In Europe, tradition is everything; at this time, the flute was tolerated as a solo instrument, but it was always questioned and criticized. In America, the audience just went along with it all. But then, America is a newer country, a child in comparison to Europe, and as such infinitely more capable of wonder and enthusiasm. One can sense this clearly as one plays—there is a sincerity, an honesty and an innate loyalty in American audiences that is truly heartwarming.

In America, music is neither *good* or *bad*, whether it be classical, jazz or the light music known as "crossover." American audiences will not turn up their noses at a concert which includes both Scott Joplin and Mozart, whereas in Europe you have to concoct a balanced recipe of a program, one that has certain known qualities and values— a certain weight, shall we say, of composers. Once you depart from the boundaries of accepted taste, you take a risk. Perhaps the Continent is catching up; a program John Steele Ritter and I gave recently in Spain included both jazz and rags by Scott Joplin as part of a classical recital, and the Barcelona crowd went wild. Slowly but surely, things are changing.

*

As the Colbert agency succeeded in booking me into better and more prestigious places around the country, a happy combination of ambition and economics helped me in New York, where it really counted. In the early 1960s, George Schutz and Jay Hoffman, a couple of fledgling concert promoters there, were trying to figure out what it would take to get younger people interested in classical music. They sensed that ticket prices for classical concerts were prohibitively high for young pockets, and they also believed that the kind of programs usually offered were not all that interesting.

New York was essentially a showcase town. A singer or a violinist had to play New York in order to establish a career, but they could rarely make a profit. It cost a great deal to put on a concert, and impresarios were interested only in funding big-name personalities. Young artists trying to break into the field had either to scrape the money together themselves or find a rich benefactor. The programs they chose for these concerts were generally designed to impress the critics and prove the artists' versatility. As a result, the works jumped from style to style across the centuries, irrespective of the musical culture shock thus inflicted on the audience.

But Schutz and Hoffman were well aware that people don't program what they listen to at home in such an illogical way: if they feel like hearing Baroque music, they might follow Bach with more Bach and perhaps even a little more Bach: an entire evening of the Brandenburg Concerti, for example. Why should the concertgoing audience be any different?

With this in mind, Schutz and Hoffman starting putting together "theme" concerts—concerts with an underlying basic subject or period—and offering tickets at reasonable prices. Lo and behold! A new generation of listeners started emerging who'd pay a couple of dollars a ticket for an evening's entertainment. Fortunately for me, this new crowd's favorite period seemed to be the Baroque. All of a sudden, Jean-Pierre Rampal became associated with "the Best of Baroque."

One of the prime reasons for this was my records. They were getting more popular, thanks in large measure to Bill Watson, the eccentric midnight-to-dawn disc jockey at WNCN in New York. Bill used to air my recordings on a regular basis on his show *Listening with Watson*. One night, when George Schutz happened to be listening to Watson's show, Bill aired the complete set of J. S. Bach's Flute and Harpsichord Sonatas that I'd made in 1962 for Erato with Robert Veyron-Lacroix. It took two full hours. At the end, Bill came on the air and, in his deep, sonorous and incredibly mellow voice said, "I enjoyed that so much I think I'll play it all over again." And he did. Schutz called Watson to find out more about this Rampal.

It wasn't long after that that George called, offering to promote a new kind of concert, featuring Rampal as the main attraction. His musical integrity quickly appealed to me: I knew that Robert and I could work with him. Schutz's first idea was a weekend of music that would be based on a real attention-getting theme: "Pieces that George Washington Might Have Listened To." The press and the audiences loved it. Soon I was playing single-theme concerts at Town Hall and Lincoln Center. I even did two straight nights—at midnight!—of the complete Handel Flute Sonatas—and nothing else. And following that, at the Midsummer Mozart Festival (which later became the incredibly popular Mostly Mozart series), all of Mozart's flute compositions. Schutz and Hoffman had started the series as a way to make use of a then non-airconditioned Philharmonic Hall; it was obviously a marvelous idea.

Like a dream come true, I at last made my Carnegie Hall debut in 1969. The evening is fixed clearly in my mind, though in some ways I can't distinguish between the memories and the event itself; I had imagined it for so long. When one walks out onto that stage, one becomes a different person—at least, that's how I felt, inspired as I was by the hall's long and awesome history. There may be lovelier auditoriums, but I find myself more entranced by this Grand Old Lady of New York concert halls than by any other.

By the end of the sixties, I had established myself in the most important city in the United States, and it was thanks to George Schutz, Jay Hoffman, and, of course, Bill Watson. I often went with my dear friend Martin Silver, an amateur flutist and librarian, to visit Bill late at night at the studio, and we would talk about music, either on the air or while he played an hour or more of Telemann Sonatas or other works for flute and harpsichord. It seems to me, thinking back, that I don't ever remember seeing him in the daytime. We stayed in touch over the years, and he always remained loyal to me and to my recordings. And he paid me a beautiful tribute, one that showed extraordinary kindness and honor: he named one of his sons Jean-Pierre.

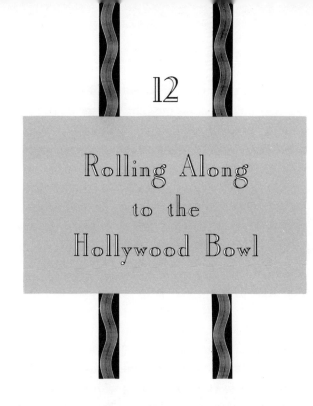

12

Rolling Along to the Hollywood Bowl

SUCCESS IN THE United States came, as it did in Europe, from work that was both *con*sistent and *per*sistent. Robert and I played everywhere we could, and were invariably invited back to the same places the following year. This regularity helped us to build and maintain an audience of well-informed—for the most part—classical music fans. But in the late seventies, things changed quite dramatically; I was suddenly able to reach even more people, ones who until then had generally avoided classical music and especially that rather esoteric instrument, the classical flute. Two events contributed to this turn-around: one was a record, totally different from the kind I usually made, and the other was a television show filmed in London with a bunch of amiable—and quite musical!—puppets.

*

One day in the early seventies I was lunching in Paris with Claude Bolling, the French jazz musician. I have known Claude for many years and have always admired his inspired piano playing and his compositions. As we finished our meal, he told me he had something he wanted me to hear. We went to his studio, where he played me a recording he'd made with Jean-Bernard Pommier, a classical pianist, for two pianos, bass and drums. It was marvelous, even if the sound of the two different pianos, one classical, one jazz, failed to provide quite enough contrast.

"Any chance you might write something like that for jazz combo and classical flute?" I asked, probably naïvely.

"Well, now that you ask . . ." Claude began, smiling.

A couple of months later, he called and said he'd got three pieces I might like to try. I went over immediately, and, with his bassist and drummer, launched into a wonderful jam session. The pieces Bolling had written ended up being called "Javanais," "Sentimentale," and "Baroque and Blue." I'd experimented slightly with jazz as a youngster at the Lycée in Marseilles, joining with a couple of friends—one who played the guitar, and the other, Christian Rasmussen, who played the piano by ear—to form a trio; we would amuse ourselves with the songs of Gershwin, Porter and Berlin. We also did some improvisations, though I must admit I wasn't very good at that, and I even learned to play a few chords on the guitar so that I could switch instruments. I was never very good at that, either. We did it for fun, and that's just what it was.

Years later in Paris, I linked up with Roger Bourdin, a great classical flutist who was also a talented composer, pianist, and a good jazz musician. Still, in our jam sessions together, he'd do the improvising. As I said, it's not something I feel I do well, and I've never been one to make a fool of myself. Amateurs can improvise, but the reason the great jazz pianists—Ellington or Teddy Wilson—were able to have their improvising styles recognized was because they *worked* at it. Just as I *worked* at becoming a classical musician, not a jazz flutist. Even though I can hold my own when playing some riffs, when I'm in the company of professional jazz players my meager improvisational talents look feeble. It was for just this reason that I always refused to record with Benny Goodman and his orchestra, even though he was constantly asking me to.

I have always liked to listen to jazz flutists such as Herbie Mann, Hubert Laws and my favorite, Jimmy Walker; in fact, these artists have made as much progress establishing the flute as a jazz instrument as I have done for the flute in classical circles. Perhaps if the flute had been more popular as a jazz instrument in my youth I would have tried a lot harder to play jazz. As it was, I never took it seriously and never feel comfortable playing straight jazz today—which is one of the main reasons why Claude Bolling's work seemed so perfect. His compositions intrigued me because they allowed me to be a classical musician—all his scores were fully notated—in a jazz environment. When we played the three pieces together they sounded so good that I wondered if we could record them. "Except," I told Claude, "there isn't enough here for a whole record. Can you write some more?" Claude said he'd see what he could come up with.

In the meantime, we taped what we'd got, using a professional studio, our own time and our own money. The idea was to make an exclusive, privately recorded disc and present it to our friends; Claude would record pure jazz on the side we'd not been able to fill, and the handsome gift would be appreciated all around. But the more we listened to ourselves, the more we believed that if Claude could expand his composition, it might reach an even greater audience. In fact, I was almost certain one of the companies I recorded for would be interested in taking on the project.

Nothing happened for a bit. And then, that summer, while I was in Nice teaching at the Academie Internationale d'Eté, Claude sent me the score for some new sections of the composition. He had also recorded the piano, bass and drum parts in Paris with his musicians, and suggested that I find a studio in Nice and dub in the flute. Pop and jazz musicians often work in this—it seems to me—disconnected manner; I never had, but was willing to give it a try. I found a superbly equipped movie recording studio called the Victorine and went to work. There were no other musicians there; just me, the technicians,

Claude's tape and the microphone. For someone used to making recordings with quartets or full orchestras, this was highly unnerving. Still, it worked surprisingly well; both Claude and I were pleased with the final result.

Since a great number of my records were issued in America and Japan by RCA, I suggested that Claude should submit the tape to them. Given RCA's already substantial catalog of my work, it seemed like a natural. But a few weeks later Claude called. "RCA doesn't want it," he said. "I got a letter from"—he read me the name— "and he says RCA isn't interested in this kind of music. He just doesn't think there's a market for it."

"Well, I'm sorry for him and RCA," I replied. "I'm sure this will do well. Try CBS: I've recorded for them a lot, too."

I occasionally think of the man at RCA who said there was no market for the Bolling Suite. I don't think he is with RCA anymore.

More than a million copies of the record have been sold since it was first released in 1975. These are very good numbers for a rock album, but extremely rare for a classical one. There's no question but that this recording changed my career and gave me a new, broader audience. I know some musicians have been jealous of what they felt was my "instant" popularity—"Oh, yes, it was the Bolling that made him a star"—but I don't think this is entirely true. By the time the piece was released, my career was already doing quite well, thank you; I was filling concert halls all over the world. Thanks particularly to my dearest Bobby Finn, my recordings at CBS were very successful. The last thing I needed was a break. In fact, recording the Bolling was something of a risk. Had the record been released in Europe first, it might have had a disastrous effect. Had the work been originally issued in France, say, the French might have felt that I had somehow denigrated my standing as a serious artist. But the American public is more intelligent and more open-minded. It could accept that a classical musician could play "crossover" music.

I've never felt it necessary to defend this recording; its success was for the most part due to Claude's absolutely inspired compositions—the Bolling Suite is, simply, wonderful music. Had that not been the case, the record would have had a quickfire success as a novelty and then vanished. But the music is exceptionally well composed, intriguing, and durable. It also opened the way for me to perform with the world's most famous singing frog and America's most notorious ham.

On a trip to New York in the early seventies, I was introduced to Jim Henson, the talented creator of the Muppets. I was an ardent fan of his creatures, and later, when he asked me to work with Kermit, Miss Piggy and the rest of the crowd I was only too delighted to accept. I couldn't imagine anything more fun.

I flew to London for three days of filming. And let me tell you: giving a concert is simple compared with all the magic that goes into making the Muppets work. But given my love for movie-making as well as the extraordinarily creative and talented Muppets handlers, it was a dream come true. I performed "Lo, Hear the Gentle Lark" with Miss Piggy, truly a diva *extraordinaire*, and several short pieces written specially for the show. These included a marvelous skit on the Pied Piper of Hamelin, in which I was beseeched by the town rats to rid the place of the children—who, in the Muppet version, were eating all the food. It was very funny indeed.

The program reached an enormous audience, almost worldwide— except for France, which was ironic and rather a pity. I could have done the dubbing myself, and my whole family would have been able to watch the show. But given the French passion for sophistication . . . well, you know what they say about prophets never being honored in their own country.

America, though, was another story. In a way it became my home base. I've come to love everything about the States, even the huge scale on which events seem to occur. "Big Is Better" is the American way, and even though the concept can be scary for a European, it turns into a delight.

Consider the Hollywood Bowl. Who would think that a flutist could perform in front of eighteen thousand people? That is BIG. I remember Zubin Mehta giving me some valuable advice when I was first scheduled to appear there: "Whatever you do, don't try to look to the back. If you start reaching for the back rows you'll lose your perspective." And he was right. The place is just enormous.

But then everything in Los Angeles is big—as it should be. This is the capital of movieland, the home of the world's dream makers. Having been a movie fan from a very early age, I was excited from the moment I first set foot in L.A. The first concert I played there, many years ago, was arranged by Henry Temianka, a superb violinist and the conductor of a chamber music ensemble. Henry became my link with the heart of the Los Angeles film community—he knew everyone—and he ferried me around to the kind of movie-star gatherings I'd only imagined as a starstruck fan.

Just on one evening out of many, I met Edward G. Robinson, Alfred Hitchcock and Anne Baxter. The party we were all attending was lavish and magnificent; I can't remember many of the conversations . . . for the most part I was speechless with awe. But I do remember spending much of my time with Anne Baxter, who over the years became a very dear friend. I told her I'd always dreamed of meeting Groucho Marx, and to my great surprise and delight, she decided to take the matter into her own hands. She spent the rest of the evening on the telephone.

Early next morning I received a telephone call. "Jean-Pierre, can you be ready in ten minutes? Groucho has agreed to see you," said Anne, a bit breathlessly.

Excited and a little nervous, I agreed, and almost before I knew it, Anne picked me up at the Beverly Hills Hotel and we drove out along Rodeo Drive.

"We've been granted a fifteen-minute audience," Anne warned me. "Jean-Pierre, you mustn't be surprised. You remember Groucho when he was young; he's an old man now, quite stooped and a little frail. I hope you won't be disappointed."

When we arrived, we were received by an elderly gentleman in his dressing gown. His mustache was, unmistakably, the real thing, but it was now pure white. We talked of many things—movies, music, Hollywood. But Groucho was mainly interested in my interest in *him*.

"Why did you want to meet an old clown like me?" he asked, without any false modesty. He really wanted to know.

"You are one of the legends of my youth," I told him. "The very fact that I can come up so close to you, sit beside you, talk to you, shake your hand—it's extraordinary."

He'd probably heard the same story a thousand times before, and he quickly changed the subject to his family's interest in music. "I was the worst musician in the bunch, you know," he said. "Chico wasn't a bad pianist, and as for Harpo—well, he really did take the harp quite seriously. Did you know he even went to Paris to study with Henriette Renié?"

I didn't know it, and I told this living icon so, but then when I looked at my watch I realized that my fifteen minutes were up.

"I've been here a quarter of an hour," I said. "Thank you so very much for your time. You don't know what this has meant to me." And I prepared to leave.

"Oh, don't worry. Stay some more." And then he added, with the inimitable Groucho wink, "I'll just charge you double."

*

Apart from the fact that Los Angeles always makes my heart pound with excitement, I have a special affection for it for another reason: it was there that I met my new partner, John Steele Ritter.

My touring schedule had increased considerably by the late seventies, and I was appearing more and more frequently as a soloist with orchestras. Sandwiched between these were the solo recitals I could fit in. In August 1974, I was scheduled to begin an orchestral tour in Los Angeles, and Ernest Fleischmann, the administrator of the Los Angeles Philharmonic, asked me if I would give a recital the day before the concert. I told him it was impossible—Robert Veyron-Lacroix couldn't possibly come all the way out to L.A. for a one-night stand, and I couldn't give a recital without a pianist. Calmly, Ernest told me not to worry; he had someone in mind who'd be perfect for the part, and I can never thank him enough for his choice.

Finding partners with whom to play is usually a matter of luck.

I'd played with Robert Veyron-Lacroix for over thirty years, and the chemistry we had onstage was something I rarely encountered with anyone else. The thought that Ernest could provide me with a partner at the last moment, for a concert to be held in the Hollywood Bowl, with perhaps a day's worth of rehearsal time, was inconceivable. But something, perhaps my innate love of adventure, moved me to agree. I trusted Ernest's judgment and his ability to sense the kind of musician with whom I could be in tune, simpatico.

I arrived from Europe the day before the concert, very jet-lagged and really just wanting to go to bed. But I decided I'd better meet this new possible partner and at least go over the program with him. John, who turned out to be only thirty-six, had studied at the Curtis Institute of Music in Philadelphia under the great Horszowski. He had received his MA in music from Northwestern University in 1974.

We rehearsed for about an hour, and despite my sleepiness I could tell that Ernest had been right: John was definitely a musician to whom I could relate. His temperament, like Robert's, is totally different from mine, yet he senses the music in the same way. He is shy and more reserved than I, but it was obvious from our first meeting that we would become friends.

I literally began to fall asleep on my feet and had to put an end to the rehearsal. But, given how well everything had gone, I wasn't concerned; I told John we'd be able to get some more practice in onstage the next day, while the microphones were being set up. Politely, John agreed, and left. What he didn't have the courage to tell me was that the microphone rehearsal was being held exactly an hour before the concert was supposed to start.

I only found this out the next day. I was mortified, but despite the fact that we barely had time to read the music through once, the performance went exceptionally well. I immediately took down John's name and telephone number. If my scheduling turned out in such a way that Robert couldn't make it to the States for a concert, I would use John. And, more and more, I did use him as my stand-in pianist; then, in 1982, Robert retired because of poor health, and I asked John if he would become my regular partner, both in the

United States and on my world tours. He readily agreed, and this musical marriage has been one of the happiest I've ever encountered.

Since then, we have crossed the United States many times over the past decade and have shared some hair-raising experiences. From near-fatal misses in Nevada and New York to plagues of insects in Illinois, we have lived the lives of two fortunate cats. I've actually lost count of how many lives we have left.

The Nevada incident was, I suppose, our own fault. We were dead set on seeing the Grand Canyon, despite the terrible weather conditions. The expedition started in Las Vegas, where we'd flown for the night. We decided to stay at the grotesquely overdone Caesar's Palace. Why not? If you are going to the cathedral of bad taste, you might just as well worship at the highest altar. Though we managed to escape the casinos only a few dollars out of pocket, our bad luck started the following day. The plane to the rim of the Grand Canyon was canceled because of the abnormally strong winds. Undeterred, we decided to rent a car. John adores driving, especially driving fast, which is paradoxical, considering his hesitant and retiring nature. So we set off on our four-hour journey, hoping to reach the canyon's edge before sunset. We arrived at this magnificent spot just as the last of the light was fading, and I suggested we stop and take photographs there and then, before checking into our hotel. This turned out to be an extremely good idea, because it was the last we saw of the Grand Canyon on that trip.

In the middle of the night, some sort of noise—actually, the *absence* of noise—woke me. In the immense stillness, there was the unmistakable soft, insulated sound of falling snow. I peered out of the window. The entire landscape was blanketed with whiteness.

The helicopter we had rented to take us through the canyon on a sightseeing flight would not even attempt to brave such conditions, and we decided we'd better give up the idea of spending a day at the Grand Canyon and fly right on to Phoenix, where we had an eight-o'clock concert date. We drove to the airport and were told, surprisingly, that our plane was likely to be on time. So we dropped off our rental car and waited. The plane was coming from Las Vegas;

it made at least three attempts to break through the thick cloud cover, but eventually the loudspeaker announced the cancellation of the flight. There was only one way to get to Phoenix: by car. John rushed back to the car-rental counter, and we were able to get hold of the same car we'd driven from Las Vegas. It was the only rental car they had.

The drive takes a good six hours under the best of conditions. It was past noon, and, although the snow had stopped falling, most of the roads were already thickly covered. The first highway we took, however, had been ploughed, and we sped along at about eighty-five miles an hour. John had studied the map and decided to turn off the main interstate and drive directly to Phoenix. All was going well until we came to what seemed a perfectly ordinary bend in the road.

"Don't brake! Don't brake!" I screamed. The road had suddenly disappeared, and we were staring at a vast and seemingly endless snowbank. John took his foot off the brake and coasted into the powder at about seventy miles an hour.

Luckily the road was straight at this point, and luckily the snow cut down our speed so that the car didn't go into a spin. We looked at each other and had memories of a previous near miss in upstate New York, when our driver had braked under similar conditions. We were racing from a concert to an airport, along a stretch of highway bounded on one side by a snow-covered bank and on the other by a ravine. We started to skid, and the driver—whom I'd already told several times to slow down—hit the brakes. That time, the car, a Lincoln Continental, went into a series of spins that I swear lasted a lifetime. I saw the ravine pass before us several times before we finally ended up in the snowbank. Barely thirty seconds later, a large truck came barreling along from the opposite direction. I think we used up two lives each on that occasion.

Now, on an Arizona highway, we ploughed through the snow at five miles an hour for what seemed an interminable age. I found myself beginning to question this life I'd chosen to lead, but as the road came back into view and we continued on our way to Phoenix, we both started to think of the concert ahead. We were late and should have stopped somewhere to tell someone what was happening. When we finally hit Phoenix, it was rush hour; we had to get clear across town, check into a hotel and change into evening clothes— all within the space of an hour. Not surprisingly, the concert organizers were quite annoyed with us. They had had no idea where we were. Rather crossly, we explained our ordeal. We had, after all, made the curtain on time. What more could they ask for? We were out of miracles for the day.

Neither John nor I were near death in Ravinia, Illinois, one hot summer, but we played under tempestuous circumstances, to say the least. On the night in question, Ravinia, which is the summer home of the Chicago Symphony Orchestra, felt like a sauna. An audience of about ten thousand people were waiting for the concert to begin, half of them under cover and half out on the lawn that stretched off into the distance beyond the stage. When we came onstage, I had the distinct sensation that I was wading through water up to my knees. Nonetheless, we started the concert. Five minutes into the first piece, the sheltered area was invaded by insects, enormous insects. It happened so quickly no one knew what was going on, and in the midst of the confusion the heavens burst open, to the screams from the people on the lawn. Like the insects, who'd obviously had the right idea from the start, everyone scurried for whatever cover they could find. We halted the concert until people had got under some kind of shelter; most of them had huddled into the many small buildings around the concert area; television screens were ready to relay the concert and we started over.

All went well until halfway through the last movement of one of the sonatas, which one I've long since forgotten, when John suddenly found himself playing solo. He looked up to find out what had happened to me. I had opened my mouth to take a breath and one of the enormous insects had flown into it. I could barely breathe, let alone play. But, as they say, the show must go on. Very stoically and with what I felt was considerable courage, I swallowed my insect and rejoined John some ten measures later. It was *not* a feast to remember!

13

Musical Cruising Around the World

TRAINS, PLANES, BOATS or whatever other form of transportation that might be needed to get me from one concert to the next are the stuff my life is made of. I play about a hundred and twenty concerts a year on four continents. That involves a great deal of traveling. But I am not complaining.

The consummate tourist, I adore visiting new places and meeting new people. I take along as many cameras as an entire family of Japanese and always try to look at things through new eyes. There's so much to see and enjoy that it's hard to believe some people become jaded and cynical when they tour the world. If you complain about Japanese food not being as good as the steak *pommes frites* in Paris, then stay in Paris! No one goes to Japan for steak *pommes frites!*

I have traveled around the world several times during the last thirty-five years. Back in the fifties, when I first took to the road as a little-known musician in search of adventure and a career, I would never have envisaged the kind of hectic schedule I have now.

My first tour took place just after the war, when I went to entertain the troops in occupied Germany. I was used to the hardships of war and the inconveniences of slow, tiring train travel, so I didn't think this trip could really count as a debut tour. In those days, even after crossing the French-German border, one noticed almost no change in the country through which we were passing. Everywhere the face of postwar Europe wore the same gray expression. This could hardly be called exciting.

When I took to the road with the members of Louis de Froment's chamber orchestra, it was a different matter. Sometimes I would call up my friend Etienne Vatelot and ask if I might borrow his large Packard. I've never understood why he always let me, because there is very little damage a group of young men won't do if left to their own devices in a borrowed car. We can't have gone too far, though, because Etienne and I are still friends; in fact, my son Jean-Jacques was at one time apprentice luthier in Etienne's workshop, and now works alongside him in Paris.

Experience proved that a flutist, a violinist and a cellist—plus their instruments—can squeeze into a car with three seats and a jump seat in the back. Etienne would see us load up, give his car a last worried pat and wish us well. Then we would head south, eating our way through France and Spain, changing tires in the mountains, playing concerts in the evenings: a troupe of latter-day pilgrims trying to top each other's stories. There were no plane or train schedules to worry about, and our only concern was finding adequate housing and a decent road. Sometimes the car would have trouble with overheating, but despite some very close calls we were always able to roll into town in time for our concerts.

Not counting physical disasters—flu, colds and suchlike—I have only missed a concert date twice in my entire life: once when I was traveling through Italy with the Trio Pasquier, and the concert organizers mixed up the dates. We arrived in Turin to find an empty hall. The second time was my fault: I had agreed to give a concert

in Toulon during what was really my vacation—probably a bit against
my will. Conscientiously, I boarded the plane from Ajaccio in Corsica
and flew to Marseilles, fully intending to fulfill my obligation, only
to find that I had got the days mixed up and was twenty-four hours
late. I made all the apologies I could, but feel embarrassed about it
even now.

Back on the road with Louis de Froment, however, we never
missed a single engagement, which rather surprised me. Oh yes, we
had plenty of adventures—what would you expect, with three strap-
ping young men all traveling together? But for the sake of propriety
and continued familial calm, I'd better leave it at that.

My first truly exotic adventure came in 1953, when a Dutch
impresario contacted Robert Veyron-Lacroix and me. He proposed
a two-month island-hopping tour of the Dutch East Indies, accompanying a young soprano named Elizabeth Lugt. We jumped at the
chance, more as tourists than as career-minded musicians. Our mission
was to entertain the Dutch expatriates working throughout the many
islands of Indonesia. The only laurels we might win from this trip
would be the ones that got tangled in our luggage as we traipsed
through the jungle.

The journey from Paris to Djakarta took three-and-a-half days.

Robert and I went from Paris to Amsterdam, where we caught
the KLM four-engine Super Constellation, a plane that even now
evokes romantic memories of early commercial aviation. Those were
the days of first-class air travel! The plane had a bar, a dance floor,
incredible food and a true party atmosphere. There were no more
than a hundred people on board, and because the journey took so
long we became a band unto ourselves. I remember dancing on the
swaying cabin deck and playing the flute as we crossed the equator.

We stopped at Bangkok for the night and disembarked with our
luggage, which gave us a chance to change into lighter clothes. This
was the first time I'd ever experienced the heat of an equatorial
monsoon season, and I never got used to it during the two months
we were there. We were always soaked with sweat and had to drink
gallons of water just to survive. The pictures Robert and I took along

the way all show us looking as if we'd been caught getting out of the shower.

In Djakarta we were met by Baron van Hittersun, the ambassador to the Dutch consulate: Robert and I were to be his guests at the residency. Of course there was no air-conditioning at that time, and the good baron saw our obvious distress.

"Don't worry, boys. I'll give you a Dutch wife for the nights. It will make things much more comfortable," he said, showing us to our rooms.

Now that's what I call hospitality! Robert and I were so dumbfounded we didn't know what to say. Elizabeth was rooming in a different house, and I wondered if they would provide her with a Dutch husband. I mumbled a quick "thank you," my face a study in bewilderment.

"This," said the baron, with a smile, "is a Dutch wife."

He held up a sheet that was attached to a large bolster. You put the sheet between your legs, he explained, to stop the flesh from chafing. It would make sleeping that much easier.

I was sure we were not the first tourists that the baron had taken pleasure in astounding.

The Indonesian tour took us from Djakarta to about fifteen different islands. Our form of transportation—little balsa-wood planes that looked barely capable of flight, let alone of weathering the prevailing conditions—was a long way away from the luxury KLM Super Constellation. On our first trip to the tiny island of Biliton we were tossed around like a nut in a Waldorf salad.

"Is it always like this?" I asked the nervous young stewardess who had come to sit beside me, perhaps because I looked the most solid of the frightened passengers. All around us, our co-travelers, mostly Chinese businessmen, were losing their lunches into white paper bags.

"Oh yes," the stewardess replied. "It's monsoon season."

I panicked. This would certainly be the first and last international tour of Rampal and Veyron-Lacroix. An inglorious end to an inglorious start. I looked at Robert, who was debating whether to reach for his paper bag.

"Do you know how many flights we have to make in these little planes?" I asked.

He shook his head.

"At least twenty-five. The law of averages can't possibly be that kind to us," I said, despairingly.

But the law *was* kind to us, as it has been several times over the years when we've been passengers in small, rickety aircraft. I'm usually more confident in planes than I am in cars driven by people I don't know, though I have had some close calls. I remember flying from Nice to a small town elsewhere on the Riviera, right through the middle of a raging storm. It was a one-engined plane, and I found myself repeating over and over again, "Why am I doing this? Why am I doing this?" And when I shared a similar hair-raising flight from Strasbourg to Montpellier with Karl Richter and Aurèle Nicolet in a tiny Fokker, I had to keep talking to Aurèle to keep my mind off imminent disaster. We looked over at Karl, whose face was ashen. He didn't say a word during the whole trip, and we never knew if he was scared to death or just contemplating Bach improvisations.

Perhaps the most excruciating experience came in the pursuit of pleasure, not performance. I was in Caracas and decided that Françoise and I should take a day off with some friends. We hired a small, one-engined plane and headed for a tiny atoll, the length of an airstrip, in the Caribbean. Both the flight out and the day itself were as relaxing as we hoped they'd be, and contentedly we loaded up for the return flight and boarded the plane. The pilot turned on the ignition; nothing happened. He kept turning, to no avail. Eventually, several people came over to the plane. Ah, I thought, they're probably going to give us a push.

One of the men then produced a cord about fifteen feet long and tied it around the propeller. The rest all stood well back and pulled. It looked exactly as if they were trying to start a lawnmower. We were all flabbergasted, but didn't say a word. The men rewound the cord and tried again. And again. Eventually the engine puttered to life. The pilot turned around in his seat and gave us a big grin. He was met with stony faces and complete silence. I resolved firmly never to take a one-engined plane again, a resolution I was forced to break by the end of the following month.

Despite the raging monsoons in Indonesia, we island-hopped successfully for two months and never again got caught in such a terrifying storm. Our greatest trial was mastering the heat and finding pianos that worked.

At some stops we were confronted with instruments that vaguely resembled pianos, but which had probably been dug up moments before in a back storeroom, covered in spiderwebs. Robert found that he would often have to rewrite Bach sonatas on the run in order to avoid ear-splitting sharps or flats. My main concerns were keeping a firm hold on a gold flute that was slippery with perspiration and finding enough oxygen in the soupy air to sustain a note. Our music-starved audiences didn't seem to care. For those who could take their eyes off Elizabeth, I think the Laurel and Hardy act of Rampal and Veyron-Lacroix—or rather, Veyron-Lacroix and Rampal, if I am to be more accurate about which of the comedians we most closely resemble—proved to be all the entertainment they required.

Indonesia was a delightful tourist experience, though, despite the climate. It was my first taste of a totally foreign culture. I tried all the food, asked thousands of questions, and took enormous pleasure in learning about local customs and meeting native Indonesians. One day Robert and I even managed to sneak into a tribal village and watch the inhabitants perform ritual dances and music; the ceremonies were held secretly, and we had to creep in quietly and make sure we weren't seen when we left.

The Indonesians were not particularly interested in our western-style music, but we were interested in theirs, especially in their gamelans—instruments made of bamboo that resembled xylophones. I actually managed to practice on one, dressed in a loincloth and a turban. My dark complexion, made darker than usual by now from the ever-present sun, gave me quite a native appearance—I even have photos to prove it!

As the time of our departure neared, we were horrified to find that all the flights from Djakarta to Europe were booked solid for the Christmas season. There was only one ticket available before December 25, and, with his usual thoughtfulness, Robert let me take it. He would endure the heat a few days longer, and I would get the chance to spend the holidays with my family. Going back also had the advantage of taking only two-and-a-half days, as we would cross the international date line in the opposite direction. Out of the frying pan and back to the hearth. I was happy to be back home. In fact, our son, Jean-Jacques, was born nine months later!

After he finished his education, Jean-Jacques occasionally joined me on tour, and I treasure these times with him. Later, as the family grew, we would more often travel en masse on our vacations. Both my children are exceptional human beings—and I don't say this just because I'm their father. They, also, have shown great devotion and love to Françoise and me.

I didn't have the chance to travel alone with my daughter, Isabelle, because she got married when she was only eighteen. She is a warm, adorable girl who, instead of becoming a careerwoman, opted to raise a family with her husband, Guillaume—a delightful young man who right away became like a second son to us. He is a bone surgeon and comes from a family of doctors, headed by his father, Professor André Dufour. Three of Guillaume's five brothers are doctors, too—it's good to have a complete hospital at home! André Dufour and his charming wife, Régine, own the property next to ours in Corsica. In fact, we bought ours because of them; we form a great "Mafia" during the summer holidays.

Jean-Jacques married Virginie Cadet de Fontenay last year, and I think she is the perfect choice for him: she adores music, she is lovely, and she and her family were immediately adopted by the Rampal-Dufour clan.

I rarely see my cousin Jacques Bec, not often enough, even though we spent our holidays together when we were young; he lives in Avignon, where he is an English teacher. His sister, Chris, lives in Paris, and we see her often. My other cousin, Claude, lives and teaches in Marseilles, and I am able to see her and her parents when I'm playing there.

Even though, in most of my travels today, I'm visiting places I've already seen, I always meet new people and have new experiences. The feeling of being at home everywhere—knowing that wherever I go I will see old friends and return to warmly remembered restaurants—is a wonderful one.

I always think of Pierre Pierlot when we talk about touring. When I would ask him where it was we played on such-and-such a day, he'd say, "Jean-Pierre, I am not very good at geography, but I can tell you the name of the restaurant where we ate. I'm a master of restaurant geography."

And he was. Restaurant geography is a preoccupation among my friends; we're in the habit of swapping great restaurants and discussing food whenever we tour. I was talking to Isaac Stern on the phone one day, and mentioned I was going to spend a week in San Francisco.

"You have time to go to Sam Wo's, Yuet Lee's and Swan's?" he asked.

"Twice each!" I replied happily.

"Oh, don't make me jealous."

Sam Wo's is a great favorite of mine: it's a hole-in-the-wall Chinese restaurant on Washington Street that makes a marvelous raw fish salad worthy of any three-star establishment—where you *don't* have to walk through the kitchen and up three rickety flights of stairs to find a table. Yuet Lee's, at the corner of Broadway and Stockton, is also superb, and Swan's is a seafood dreamland. None of these places is chic, but they share a place in the collective restaurant address book of many of my friends.

My world, I'm happy to say, is dotted with such shared experiences. I'm sure I could write an excellent international restaurant guide that would take people from the best three-star *Guide Michelin* establishments through the back streets of Tokyo to the tiny *yakitori* houses frequented only by the Japanese themselves. I remember dragging a more-than-willing Vera and Isaac Stern on just such an adventure through Tokyo. And I also remember trying to persuade them to get up at five in the morning to go down to the fish market for what must surely be the best sushi in the world, which we ate standing at the little wharfside kiosks.

People think of me as a typical French gourmet: "Oh, he's very much a gourmet, he adores food," they say, and I do. I love *all* good food: French, Japanese, Greek, Hungarian, Indian, Vietnamese—you name it, I'll eat it. I can think of only one place in the world where I didn't eat well, and that was Egypt. My wife and I were touring the tombs and pyramids, and I must say I didn't have a single decent meal the whole time there. Egypt was a godsend when it came to my constant battle with an ever-expanding waistline—the curse of the gourmand—because it's the only country I know where I find it easy to stay on a diet.

Everywhere else, I eat well. Most of all I love the *cuisine populaire*— home-style cooking. I like going to simple, unpretentious restaurants where the atmosphere is often as warm and spicy as the food being prepared. The United States doesn't really have a great indigenous cuisine, and I don't think I will offend anyone by saying so. A simple hamburger or cheeseburger cooked on an open grill in the garden of some of my friends' houses is a marvel for me, as good as any fine French dish. And a superb lobster in Massachusetts or fresh crab in San Francisco is pure poetry. And don't forget the meat. Prime ribs *au jus* in the United States cannot be beaten anywhere in the world. I am very pleased that my good friend Paul Bocuse (it's superfluous to say his restaurant near Lyons is one of the most famous of all temples of culinary delights) shares my own taste for what he calls *la cuisine de la rue*, especially in Japan, where he combs the streets to find the little mobile restaurants that serve small and marvelous delicacies. *La cuisine de la rue*—it's there you will find the heart of a nation.

More important to me than the restaurants themselves are the people with whom I share the meals and who make certain places more memorable than others. For me, fine dining and fine music have always gone together. I could very well have called this book *Great Meals I Have Shared Around the World*, because for every concert I have played there has generally been a remarkable culinary experience to accompany it. And the recipe for enjoyment always includes two basic ingredients: friends and music.

A favorite and unforgettable memory of mine is of a day in London when Claudio Scimone, the director of I Solisti Veneti, whom I first met in Padua, managed to eat two lunches and a dinner and in between conduct a Vivaldi-Mozart concert.

We had lunch reservations at Chez Prunier, one of London's best French restaurants, but we were early and decided to drop into a sushi bar across the mews to whet our appetites. Never really able to restrain ourselves when it comes to good food, Claudio, Edward Beckett, the flutist nephew of Samuel Beckett, and I plunged into the sushi with great gusto. The three of us were fairly large men, and Eduardo Farina, the very thin harpsichordist of the group, who found himself sandwiched between us, had no idea what to do when confronted with all this food and the prospect of more to come. He was completely overwhelmed when, having finished mountains of sushi, Claudio looked at his watch and realized he still had time to make his Chez Prunier reservation. Even I was astounded. I raised the white flag and retreated to take my pre-concert nap. I caught up with Claudio onstage, and we gave a marvelous performance. Then we went on to *another* feast, and as he tucked into his third big meal of the day, Claudio told me about the suberb meal I'd missed. Now, as we get older, we are all more circumspect about our eating habits— and I know that Claudio follows a strict diet. I'm sure, however, he won't mind my revealing his past culinary conquests.

Not all good meals are shared in restaurants. Some of my greatest musician friends are also great chefs: Sasha Schneider, for example, who can produce a wonderful non-Christmas Christmas dinner of calf's liver and onions—and did so for me one year in New York. And the guitarist Alexandre Lagoya, with whom I play all over the world, is also a dedicated chef, who has a superb kitchen with an old-fashioned spit. One of his specialties is sea bass cooked whole under a mountain of sea salt. The fish stews in its own juices and when you remove the salt, all the flavor remains in the fish. Alexandre then makes a sauce with crème fraîche and an enormous quantity of caviar, which is served with the fish. I don't think I'm giving away his secret recipe by describing this, because I couldn't possibly guess the amounts—or even the names—of all the herbs and spices he throws into the pot.

Dining *chez* Georges Barboteu is also an extraordinary experience. I have known Georges since my early days in Paris. He is a great horn player, a great friend, and a great gourmet, who has a joviality that is hard to match. Among his other talents, which include a wonderful ability to mimic famous conductors, is a mouth-watering dish of freshly made angel hair pasta in a lobster sauce, followed by the lobsters themselves. What a meal!

Visiting Spain, for example, was made perfect for me because of the hospitality of Marquese Luis de Bolarque, a gentleman who knew every nook and cranny of his country. I met him in Paris in 1950, and he invited me to come and play with an orchestra he sponsored in Madrid. He took me to some of the best three-star restaurants and to delightful country taverns where the gypsies played their heart-stopping, emotional music. Once, driving through the countryside, we turned off the road on to what was little more than a dirt track and came to a village Luis knew well. He took me into the local church, and there, in the middle of this almost unknown town, was a stunning El Greco. For me, Spain *means* Luis de Bolarque, and though we lost touch with each other when he moved to Bonn to become Spanish ambassador to Germany, and died soon after that, he will always live on in my mind as my guide to Spain.

The Mediterranean is a sea of memories. Each summer since 1968, family, friends and I have taken part in concerts aboard the cruise ships *Renaissance* and *Mermoz* for a musical whirl around the Mediterranean. These cruises were the brainchild of a lively Hungarian named André Borocz, who also organized the Menton Festival. A cruise is perhaps the most relaxed kind of concert schedule one can have. You are on a boat with musicians, friends and several hundred music lovers. You meet your audience—and, because it's a captive one, it stays the same every day!—and get to know it; this makes every performance something of a family affair, much more so than a regular concert.

The first cruise in 1968 was a trial balloon. The concert schedules were all planned in advance, and we played and rehearsed at specified hours. But the holiday atmosphere and the warm geniality that existed among the musicians soon got things going far less formally. We would generally meet on the first day of the cruise and discuss the kind of things we would like to play and the sort of ensembles we would like to form. For example, Isaac Stern and I might link up with Slava Rostropovich for an evening of trios.

Françoise generally comes with me on these trips, and sometimes other members of the family, too. You eat, swim in the pool by day and play music by night. The weather is usually beautiful, and the food extraordinary; in fact, one of the main temptations is to eat far too much. Isaac has joined these musical cruises many times, as has Slava, Maurice André and Arthur Rubinstein. Sasha Schneider has come along, as has Pierre Pierlot and Alexandre Lagoya. And the list gets longer as the years go on: I've been doing it myself now for seventeen years.

I have what must be collectors' items—home movies of us at play that go back to the days when video camera recorders didn't exist. I'd make a appropriate soundtrack after the event and synchronize the image with the music. I wonder if anyone else has ever witnessed—not to say captured on film—Slava Rostropovich attempting a double pirouette with a ballerina from the Paris Opera Ballet? Or the Rostropovich-Stern-André-Rampal quartet making waves in a decktop pool?

Sometimes I gather my friends together in my home on Avenue Mozart and we relive those days, watching the thousands of feet of film I've taken over the years that have captured forever my persistent peregrinations. Staying at home can be fun, too—but I don't think I'll ever be cured of my addiction to travel.

14

Prague, Tokyo and New York:

Of Singing Tenor, Eating Sushi and Meeting Friends

I HAVE TRAVELED AROUND the world many times, yet three countries have a special place in my heart: Czechoslovakia, Japan, and, of course, the United States. In Prague I met a man who, over the years, came to be almost a musical mentor for me. The Japanese took to me as quickly and as warmly as I took to them, and I shall never forget my first welcome there. And I have spent so much time in the United States that I often think of it as my second home—particularly New York, which is for me a vibrant, energizing city and one to which I feel especially akin because it was the first place I visited in the United States. But Boston, Chicago, Los Angeles—the list could go on and on—are all special to me, each in its own way.

*

If I play Carl Philipp Emanuel Bach well, it is thanks to Milan Munclinger, a Czech I met in 1956. Milan died at the beginning of

1986, and my recordings of the C.P.E. Bach Concerti made after that time are dedicated to his memory. I have not returned to Prague since his death, and I know that any visit I make there in the future will find me in a different city. For me, Prague is bound up with my memories of Milan, his friends and our musical merrymaking.

Prague is also special to me because it was the first city I visited behind the iron curtain, as well as the place in which I heard Slava Rostropovich for the first time; he was giving the premiere outside Russia of Prokofiev's Sinfonia Concertante. I had never before heard a cellist play with such apparent ease: his sound was extraordinary, and his technique truly fabulous. Prague was also where I first met Jindřich Feld, a young composer who has written numerous wonderful pieces for me, including the concerto that inspired Khachaturian to suggest I transcribe his Violin Concerto for the flute.

What strikes anyone visiting Prague for the first time is its untouched beauty. The city has never been bombed; it remains a living memorial to the eighteenth century—Mozart's century. Mozart was happy in Prague; it was the kind of city that welcomed the high spirits and practical jokes he loved. Had he stayed in Prague, perhaps he would not have come to such an ignominious end. But that was not his destiny. In Prague in 1956, I always had the impression that I might meet Mozart around the next corner. I felt closer to him there than anywhere else. When Miloš Forman made *Amadeus*, it was delightful to see that he used Prague, rather than Vienna, as his setting. The spirit of Mozart is very much alive there.

In 1956, the political situation was worse than it is today, and the artistic community was hounded by politics and repression. Hungary, Czechoslovakia's neighbor, had failed to throw off the severe dictates of the Moscow regime, and the Czechs were chastened and disturbed by the news of the fighting in Budapest. But the musical life of Prague continued.

Milan Munclinger lived on the edge of the accepted musical world; he was not wholeheartedly welcomed into the community, but because of his fine flute playing and his brilliant conducting he found work with the various Prague chamber orchestras. He was comparatively unknown, and I would never have met him through my official guides and translators. But he had attended a concert of mine and decided he wanted to meet me. He turned up at my hotel.

"I came to meet you, to talk with you, and to play together," he said, in the most extraordinary French accent I had ever heard. He spoke a scholarly French that came directly off the pages of Voltaire, and which sounded otherworldly and charming. His Italian was even more amusing. He had never had a formal lesson in the language in his life, but he knew all the great Italian operas by heart. His Italian conversations were a mixture of highflown drama and wild imperatives that never failed to reduce his audience to helpless laughter. Imagine using the libretto of *Don Giovanni* or *Aïda* to negotiate your way around Rome! Our rapport was immediate.

Milan was an expert on the Rococo period, a period that was rife with ornamentation, elegant cadenzas and complicated improvisations. His life, in contrast to the highly embellished style of the music he loved, was very simple, almost hermetic. Food was important only insofar as it was a necessity of life. He loved fine dining, but was often totally overwhelmed by rich meals. Later, when I invited him to teach at the Académie Internationale d'Eté in Nice, where I was something of a founding father, he came with delight but begged me not to force him to join me and my friends each night for the sumptuous feasts we all enjoyed so much.

"My stomach and my spirit are not used to such abundance and variety," he said. "If I ate like this for a week I would not recognize myself afterward, either in body or mind. I wouldn't be Milan anymore. I would lose my personality."

That personality, of which he was fiercely proud, was a marvelous mixture of love of life and love of music. He had a vibrant circle of friends in Prague, musicians, composers, singers, all of whom became my friends too. And he was a tremendous party-giver, who loved to organize musical evenings. One of these will always remain in my memory. It was a tenors' evening: everyone who came, regardless of who he was or what he played, had to sing a tenor aria.

Milan invited two basses from the Prague Opera, who duly

stretched their vocal cords and delighted everyone. Watching a bass reach for a high F can be an excruciatingly funny experience. Watching a flutist struggling to sing that wonderful aria "Celeste Aïda" had a similar effect on the crowd. It was a veritable massacre of Verdi's genius.

A latecomer to this wild event was Jendřich Feld, whom I met the first time I played in Prague, when he had approached me after the concert, carrying a huge musical score. He was polite but firm.

"Mr. Rampal, this is a concerto I have written for the flute. I would like you to look at it. You do not have to play it; you do not even have to tell me what you think of it, but it is my duty as a composer to show my music to a musician who can play it."

I was stunned by his attitude, and unquestioningly took the bundle of music he handed me back to my hotel. When I got home, I read through the score: it was a dramatic, romantic piece in the style of Prokofiev that gave the flute a powerful voice. When the Czech Philharmonic Orchestra called to invite me back to Prague, I agreed on the stipulation that I could premiere the Feld Concerto.

But back in Prague, on the night of the tenors' "concert," Jindřich pleaded laryngitis. He had, however, come up with a replacement for his voice—an ocarina—and had composed an outlandishly ribald theme and variations based on a famous Czech drinking song that had us laughing heartily over our steins—our many steins—of pilsner.

Milan was also responsible for my only other foray into operatic mortification. He and I had been doing a recording session in a Prague studio, and when it was over we went to his home, which contained a nearly professional recording setup—his pride and joy. Milan suggested that we experiment, and started playing around with "Là ci darem la mano," the lovely duet between Zerlina and the Don from Mozart's *Don Giovanni*. Somehow I was coaxed into recording both voices—*sans* flute! I sang the soprano part of Zerlina twice as slowly and an octave lower than normal, and Milan later speeded up the tape and overdubbed it on to my rendition of the baritone part. Needless to say, the experiment was tremendous fun, but neither Domingo nor Pavarotti has anything to worry about, nor Joan Suth-

erland or Kathleen Battle, for that matter: I think—at least I hope—
the recording is lost forever.

Milan was exactly my age, and he was like a brother to me. I
respected both his musical integrity and his musical pride. When he
approached a work by Bach or Handel, he would make it seem as if
the composer were alive. Music played this way can never sound
dead; it can never sound academic or dry. Any knowledge or ability
to understand and to play Rococo music—and especially that of
C. P. E. Bach—I credit to my mentor, Milan, and lay my thanks at
his feet.

*

When I arrived at Haneda airport in Tokyo, I couldn't believe my
eyes. There were hundreds of people waving banners emblazoned
"Welcome, Mr. Rampal." An exquisite Japanese girl dressed in a
kimono came forward and handed me flowers. Cameras were going
off all over the place. And I had never been to Japan before.

My records had preceded me, and the flute has always been a
favorite instrument in the Land of the Rising Sun—indeed, I think
of the flute as one of the three viruses the Japanese can't get rid of,
the other two being the telephone and the camera. Nevertheless, I
was astonished and warmed by the tremendous welcome. It seemed
as if the Japanese somehow sensed that I would take to their country,
and they were there to show me how.

From Day One, I tried to live the life of a Japanese. I think I am
basically adventurous by nature, and all the newness in Japan excited
me; I wanted to try *everything* Japanese. I reserved a Japanese suite
with tatami at the Okura Hotel in Tokyo. I tried every kind of food
that was placed before me, even though it sometimes looked me back
straight in the eye. I was "tatami-ized" very quickly, and perhaps
that is why people cottoned on to me: I was seduced by their customs,
their food and their music.

The Okura Hotel is probably one of the four best hotels I have
ever stayed in anywhere in the world. Only the Hotel Oriental in
Bangkok and the Mandarin and the Peninsula in Hong Kong are in

the same category. So, if possible, I try to stay at the Okura and I always ask for one of the Japanese suites, which are on the seventh floor. I had one on my very first visit, and was so impressed with its beauty that I couldn't wait for Françoise to join me later in the week, so that I could show her around. I was also quite impressed with my rapid ability to master the Japanese way of life, and wanted to show off that skill to Françoise, too.

Like me, she received a wonderful reception at Haneda airport, and then made her way to the Okura. A little pond, with a delicate bridge arching over it, faces you as you enter the suite. The flowers, elegantly and discreetly arranged throughout the rooms, are beautiful, and there are carvings and exquisite furnishings everywhere. It all took Françoise's breath away.

On the Sunday following her arrival, we found ourselves alone. The guides, who normally escort you everywhere, always take Sunday off, leaving their charges to their own devices. I felt sufficiently "tatami-ized" to suggest that Françoise and I tackle a restaurant in the Ginza, the heart of the Tokyo shopping district.

"But how will we manage? You don't speak Japanese," she said.

"Don't worry," I replied. "Have you ever known me at a loss for words in a restaurant?"

To which, of course, she had no reply, and we set off immediately.

The first few dishes arrived just as I'd expected—and were exactly what I'd ordered.

"Now I think we'll have some oysters," I said.

"Good idea!" exclaimed Françoise. "What's the Japanese for 'oyster'?"

"You'll see."

Our lovely Japanese waitress came over to the table.

"*Kaki*," I said with great confidence, pronouncing it as you would "cocky"—very appropriate for the situation.

Moments later the young lady returned with a plate of persimmons.

I shook my head. "*Kaki*," I tried again.

And the girl returned with even more persimmons. By this time, Françoise was almost hysterical. I, on the other hand, was getting quite hot under the collar and was determined not to be beaten.

"Your Japanese *is* impressive," said Françoise, as yet a third plate of persimmons arrived. Exasperated, I tried one more time, my voice trailing off at the end of the word.

"*Kaki*," I said, with a falling accent on the final syllable.

"Ah," said the waitress. "*Kaki*," she went on, mimicking my accent. She put her hands together to imitate an oyster.

I started nodding wildly. Yes, oysters, we want oysters! But the little waitress shook her head. They were out of oysters that day.

So we never got our *kaki*, but I did manage to climb back a little in Françoise's estimation as we returned to the Okura and our perfect Japanese suite.

If I am unable to stay at the Okura, my second choice is the Imperial. It is a fine establishment, luxurious and wonderfully run, and it has the added advantage of being within two hundred yards of Negishi Camera in the Sukiyabashi Shopping Center. On my first trip to Japan, Ben Joppe, the head of Philips Records, introduced me to Mr. Negishi, and I go back to visit him every time I am in Tokyo. I am as fascinated by cameras as the Japanese themselves, and have collected so many different kinds over the years that our apartment on the Avenue Mozart could be converted into a camera shop. There is a whole room filled with equipment and films and lenses, and much of it is thanks to Mr. Negishi. I must be one of his best clients. Never a week goes by when I'm in Tokyo that I don't find myself talking to Mr. Negishi, either with film to be processed, or a camera part to be repaired, or a new tripod to buy. Other flutists come to Japan to try out all the wonderful flutes they make there—and sometimes I do that, too—but my real passion is for cameras.

My introduction to Japan came from a former student and wonderful flutist, Hirohito Kato—who died tragically while climbing in the Alps. It was he who suggested I be invited to play in Japan. My Japanese impresario, Hiroshi Kobayashi, organized that visit. All my tours since then have gone well, and Kobayashi quickly became a delightful friend. The Japanese public is very attached to the flute and very loyal to the artists who play it. I started performing Japanese folk music the moment I got to Japan, and the very first year I was there made a recording of popular airs, including "Sakura, Sakura" and "Haru no Umi," a wonderful piece for flute and the Japanese stringed instrument called the koto. The first piece is about cherry blossoms, the second means "the sea in springtime." I include Japanese music in each recital I give there, and people say I "breathe" the music like a Japanese.

The most successful record I ever released in Japan was probably a recording of popular Japanese melodies for flute and harp that I made in the late sixties with Lily Laskine. Lily had never been to Japan—she rarely liked to set foot outside France—and at the beginning of the recording session in Paris, she asked me for advice on how the music should sound. I don't think I'd played more than a couple of bars before she joined in; it was as if she'd been playing Japanese music all her life. It came to her so naturally that the Japanese could not believe she was Occidental—and, what's more, an Occidental who'd never once set foot in the Orient. The record was so popular it was named "Record-of-the-Year" in Japan, the award being made at the Japanese pavilion at the 1970 World's Fair in Tokyo. The themes began to be used as introductory pieces for television and radio programs, as well as to accompany announcements at the airport.

There is also a sort of Rampal Fan Club in Yokohama that was started by a flutist who has since become a good friend. His name is Ei-ichi Akahoshi, and we met during my first visit. It all came about with an invitation to play in Yokohama. After my concerts, Ei-ichi would invite his flute-playing friends and his students to a wonderful meal, and, little by little, our group took on a life of its own. One year he realized I had a free day after my Yokohama concert, and asked me if he could organize a little excursion to a fishing village nearby. We had a great time. Now, whenever I visit Yokohama, Ei-ichi arranges a trip. He hires two railway carriages, and off we go to a Japanese inn near the sea and have a fishing party. We spend the day fishing for *aji*, a kind of mackerel, going out in boats and usually being quite successful. We don't eat what we catch, because there isn't the time to prepare it, but we have an enormous feast nevertheless—after our baths, of course. Usually about thirty people come, all of whom are Japanese except for me and John Steele Ritter, who has joined us on several occasions. It is an incredible banquet: the dining table is decorated with fish and festooned with flowers so that it resembles a painting, and one is almost afraid to touch anything for fear of spoiling such a pretty arrangement. Needless to say, these trepidations are quickly overcome. Later, there is music. One year, we even had someone bring a little spinet, so we could play flute and harpsichord duets. You can't imagine how much fun it is to eat fresh fish surrounded by thirty Japanese flutists!

It is moments like these that make a country very special. The Japanese can be extremely reserved when they are attending a concert, however: they don't applaud during the recital, even at the conclusion of a piece, so you have be quite patient and wait to see what kind of reception you are going to get when the concert's over. I have for years now received a warm welcome in Japan, and when I return to the stage to give an encore I usually choose a Japanese popular song. From that very first recording I made of "Sakura, Sakura," it seems that a cult has grown up. I just have to play the first few notes and the audience starts to clap enthusiastically, as if I were Frank Sinatra breaking into "My Way." It's an extraordinary feeling for a classical musician.

*

In 1954, I was making my way across the Atlantic en route to Canada and decided to ask for a tourist visa to the United States, so that I could take advantage of a route that would allow me to spend half a day in New York. The idea excited me tremendously. The images of New York's lofty skyline and immense buildings had always attracted me. I love cities, and always try to stay in the center of them when on tour. The suburbs are for the birds. If I want to go to the country, I go *way* into the country, but if I'm going to perform in a city, then you will always find me in a hotel nearest the center. And in 1954, when I arrived at Idlewild airport, as Kennedy was then called, I wanted to make for the heart of New York as quickly as possible.

"Times Square," I told the taxi driver. And we sped across Queens toward Manhattan. Then, for three hours, I walked up and down streets whose names had been just that—names—until then. Fifth Avenue, Broadway, Herald Square. My neck ached and my finger was tired from pushing the camera button so often, but I was extremely happy. I knew New York was just waiting to become my second home.

And over the years, it has. I am still as much in love with the city as ever, even though now I see it for what it is. I see the excitement and I see the violence; I see the bright lights and I see the poverty. There is a grandeur about the towering architecture that both over-whelms me and weighs me down, but I find it very beautiful. I love New York on its own terms. Perhaps if I lived there year round, I might tire of the pace, but when I'm there for a visit, it's invigorating and tremendous fun. It is the home of Carnegie Hall. It is, as the song says, a town that never closes, and it is a town full of warm, appreciative audiences. What more could a musician want?

I have scores and scores of friends in New York, so many that I can rarely see them all in one visit. My dressing room used to get so crowded that, instead of organizing visits to special restaurants for me after a concert, my friends would volunteer to host parties. Sometimes my producer George Schutz would do the honors. Bobby Finn and Pierre Bourdain were also particularly kind over the years. Pierre died suddenly in 1987; I had met him through Bobby, and he immediately became one of my closest friends. He had a sensitivity to music that went to the very heart of the matter. If Pierre said he liked a concert, then you knew it had gone well. I respected his opinion completely. His musical taste never erred, and his music shop, Orpheus, on Lexington Avenue, always carried the best collection of

CDs anywhere. It saddens me that he is no longer in New York, but I have wonderful memories of our times together, times that are bound up with music and the city.

*

If I am not celebrating after a concert at the house of a friend, then I am celebrating with friends at a restaurant. I have many favorites in New York—of course, I love the great French restaurants, including Lutèce, La Côte Basque, and Le Bourgogne, but I also love places that are less *haut*, too. When I first started going to Le Refuge, for example, it was a small place run by a delightful Frenchman, Pierre Saint-Denis. Pierre is a superb cook, who has a wonderfully simple way with food. I always send my friends to Le Refuge. Even after Pierre changed his location and the restaurant became extremely chic, I still kept going there. Pierre and I are great friends, and I am godfather to his youngest child. Pierre is also a very good amateur flutist, so we have more than just fine dining in common.

There is, however, one restaurant in New York that I won't go to: the Russian Tea Room. They can take their caviar and blinis and serve them to all the stars in town, but they won't serve them to me—no matter how much I crave caviar. One evening, when I was supposed to be dining there, I was forced to change my plans. I popped into the restaurant to find my dinner guests so that I could explain why I was unable to join them. It was in the middle of winter, and I was wearing a bulky fur coat. As I spun through the revolving doors and tried to make my way to my friends' table, the maître d' barred my way.

"I'm sorry, sir, but you can't go into the dining room in your coat. Could you check it, please?" It didn't sound much like a request to me.

"I've just got to say a couple of words to my friends and I'll leave," I explained.

"You can't go into the dining room dressed like that," he persisted.

At this point, I became angry. The restaurant is right next to Carnegie Hall, and you'd think they'd recognize some of the artists who play there regularly and at least make an attempt to be polite. I don't like to throw my weight around—it can be dangerous for those in the immediate vicinity—but on this occasion the supercilious mâitre d' had made me very angry.

"Excuse me," I said and pushed past him, coat and all. And on the way out I pushed past him again, without a word. I never went back. Ever.

I prefer friendly, accommodating establishments, and that is just what Elaine Kaufman provides over on Second Avenue and Eighty-eighth Street. My dear friends James and Kedakai Lipton first introduced me to Elaine's. She serves very good food indeed, and plenty of friendly warmth to go along with it. It is also a place where I get to see lots of my friends. A table seems to be permanently reserved for Woody Allen, and it's always fun to run into him. We both play wind instruments, after all, and we both love the movies!

And somehow, despite the crowds, Elaine always seems to find a table for me whenever I come in. The place may be packed to the doors, but she just says, "Wait five minutes," and in less than three, my party of twelve will be seated. I have never been able to figure out how she does it.

It was like that the night I introduced Luciano Pavarotti to Elaine's. My son, Jean-Jacques, and I had been to hear him give a Madison Square Garden concert, which featured Andrea Griminelli, my former student and a very fine flutist. Andrea had originally introduced me to Pavarotti. Luciano invited us backstage after the event. He said there was going to be a reception.

As usual, the greenroom filled up as Luciano was changing, and I happened to notice that what little there was of the buffet was fast disappearing. Like most artists, Luciano doesn't eat before a concert.

"He is going to be hungry. And he is going to be angry when he sees how little food there is," I told Jean-Jacques. "We've got to have a back-up plan."

So when Luciano came into the room, I immediately pulled him aside.

"There isn't enough food here to satisfy a Mimi!"

"But where can we go? Even Sardi's will be closed by now," he said sadly.

"Say your hellos and good-byes, and I'll take you to Elaine's."

"Where's that?"

"You've never been there?" I asked in surprise. "Don't worry. You'll have a good time. It's Italian."

Moments later we were seated in the middle of Elaine's, pondering the menu.

"*Vongole al forno!*" cried Luciano.

The first dozen clams arrived, and Luciano wolfed them down the way you'd expect a tenor who'd performed before forty-five thousand people would.

"*Vongole al forno!*" he cried again.

In no time at all, Luciano had managed to consume about four dozen of the delicious little beasts. Jean-Jacques and Andrea looked on, wide-eyed. Actually, that's only about twenty-four mouthfuls. And I must admit that four dozen clams don't frighten me in the least, either.

Talking of shellfish reminds me of Boston, and in particular of Anthony's Pier 4. I don't think there is another restaurant in the world where you can get a twelve-pound lobster that tastes so good— or a twelve-pound lobster at all, for that matter! Though I usually just take the shuttle from New York to Boston when I have one-night engagements there, I always have time to have dinner at Pier 4. Once, when I was playing at the Tanglewood Festival in the Berkshires, I craved lobster so much that I decided to make the two-hour drive into Boston just for the afternoon. I wanted to share this experience with my friends and son, so Jean-Jacques, John Ritter, Pierre Bourdain and Bobby Finn joined the expedition. We were driving along the Massachusetts Turnpike at a quite impatient eighty-five miles an hour when it occurred to me that the speed limit isn't the same in the United States as it is in Europe.

"How fast can I go?" I asked John, lobsters clearly on my mind.

"Fifty-five," said John.

"What will happen if I get caught speeding?"

"They'll probably take away your license and fine you."

"Oh, that's okay then," I said, relieved.

"Why?" John asked.

"I don't have my license."

Bobby and John looked at each other incredulously.

"Slow down, Jean-Pierre," they blurted out simultaneously.

But, as I said, I had lobsters on my mind, and we continued on to Boston at a speed well over the legal limit. (The lobsters were, of course, worth it.)

But Boston means more to me than just lobsters. There's Symphony Hall and the wonderful Boston Symphony Orchestra. Whenever I play with them, I feel as if I'm playing with close friends. I also have a special fondness for Boston because I have a child from there: my flute. I should say children, as I have four gold flutes from William S. Haynes & Co., whose headquarters are in Boston. Ever since Lola Haynes begged me to take one of the flutes that Lewis Deveau made back in the late fifties, I have remained faithful to Haynes flutes, and whenever I'm in town I try to visit the company, and Lew Deveau, who is now its president.

It would take too long to go through an entire list of all the towns in the United States that I love, but I will mention just three more: Chicago, San Francisco and Atlanta. Chicago has a marvelous concert hall. Whenever I play there, the audience always overflows onto chairs onstage, for the Chicago public is consistently warm and welcoming. Among the many friends I have there, Elizabeth Stein is one of the dearest. She's a delightful character with a great personality, and a very warm hostess. The face of San Francisco has changed for me because my old friend the surgeon Coleman Citret died a couple of years ago, but I will never forget the wonderful times I had with him and his family, who opened their home so warmly to me.

Up until about ten years ago, there was only one major city in the United States where I had not played: Atlanta. This bothered me. I asked George Schutz why I had never been invited there, but he didn't have an answer.

"Let's see what we can do about it," he said, as usual taking up the challenge of an untapped market. George has always delighted in booking me into places where I have never played. We both wondered how Atlanta had escaped my schedule for so long.

A few weeks later, George called me.

"I think you're going to love this one, Jean-Pierre," he said. "I've booked the Fox Theatre, the very same place where they premiered *Gone with the Wind*."

"That's wonderful—but isn't it very large?" I replied.

"Four thousand seats," said George.

"That's quite a lot for a first concert, isn't it?"

"Don't worry. I bet there'll be chairs onstage." This was one of George Schutz's favorite expressions. Whenever I worried about appearing in a new town, George would always cheer me up by saying they were going to have to sell stage seats, and would that bother me?

I looked forward to my Atlanta debut. New towns and new people are always special. The moment when one steps onstage and tries to take in the full resonance of the new hall; the moment when, suddenly, one *knows* one has won over the audience; the moment, at the end, when applause is all around—all this is the stuff performing is made of. And a four-thousand seat hall that had seen Clark Gable and Vivien Leigh take a bow was a place in which I was very excited to be.

The day before the concert, just after I arrived in Atlanta, I fell ill with a flu-like bug that took away all my energy. There was no possibility of performing, and I was laid so low the doctors decided I'd better go straight back to New York for some tests. The concert would have to be cancelled. I was very disappointed, but there was nothing I could do about it. George was probably more disappointed than I was: as promoter of the concert, he stood to lose a good deal of money.

"Is there any way we can reschedule?" he asked me.

"I hope so," was all I could manage to mutter from my hospital bed. Things had turned out pretty bad, and I'd had to cancel more than just that concert in Atlanta. "Maybe in a couple of months."

But I recovered surprisingly quickly, and there was an opening in the Fox Theatre schedule. The public had not turned in their tickets en masse, which pleased George, and when it finally took place, my debut in Atlanta was a sell-out. Since then I have returned many times, and I am always grateful to the Atlanta public for forgiving me my first cancellation and having the faith to hold on to their tickets.

During my tours in the States, the familiar faces of orchestral managements and players—frequently surfacing in changing locales— have brightened my life. I first met Peter Pastreich in St. Louis, and now he is executive director of the San Francisco Symphony. Gideon Toeplitz, whom I met when he was a child in Tel Aviv (his father was the principal flutist of the Israel Philharmonic), was assistant manager with the Boston Symphony, then with the Houston Symphony and now with the Pittsburgh. These two men, among many others, have become dear friends, and whenever I visit the cities where they live they make me feel very much at home.

I have read a lot of autobiographies, but until I began writing my own I never realized how much agony the shortage of space can cause. One has to omit hundreds and hundreds of people—those who have shown particular kindnesses, both great and small. The thought of facing these people after this book is published fills me with dread; I beg their forgiveness. Friends, fellow musicians, conductors, concert promoters and their staffs, students, hosts and hostesses . . . I have been especially blessed by their thoughtfulness and devotion.

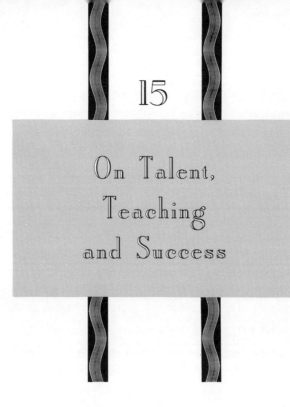

15

On Talent, Teaching and Success

TO PLAY A MUSICAL instrument, you need the discipline to work and study. To play a musical instrument extremely well, you need talent. And to make a career playing a musical instrument, you need all of the above, plus a little luck.

Talent is a gift, and it comes from nature. There are people who are born with more talent than others. That is the absolute law of inequality: it may not be just, but there is no way of redistributing talent. Fortunately or unfortunately, we are not cars coming off a production line. We may all have the same basic bodies, but we all perform differently, and that, to my mind, makes the world a more interesting place.

As often as not, the most talented people are not always the ones who succeed. It sometimes so happens that they do not have that special quirk of nature—the ability to truly *work* with their talent— that permits them to use it well. This is almost as unfair as having no talent at all. The talented ones, those who also work hard, are the ones most likely to make a success of a musical career. One must, however, always remember to add luck to the formula. Without this magic ingredient, talent and hard work can often amount to nothing.

Luck, as my father always said, comes to those who are ready for it. You have to know how to take advantage of your talent and hard work. If you don't believe you are a lucky person, you will never get that big opportunity, no matter how great your talent. And if you are lucky enough to be given a break, I think you also need love to make the most of the opportunity—the love of and for the public. The people listening to you must be aware that you love them and you want them to love you in return. I have always felt this emotion onstage; it is a special kind of symbiosis, one that allows you to be in contact with your audience.

Talent, hard work, luck and love: the scales are loaded on the side of talent and hard work, but without a sprinkling of luck and a large helping of love, no career stands a chance. All this, of course, is easy to say, but in the unjust world in which we live it is not enough to announce: "I have talent! I have energy! I have love for the public and they will love me! I will have luck because I believe in luck!"

I think you have to be born with these talents and this luck. You can see people who start their lives as simple farmers who work with their hands, one beside the other, and then, suddenly, and it seems for no reason at all, one becomes a success story. He opens his own factories and becomes a boss. You never know why this happens to one man and not to another. Life is not terribly fair. Criminals go without punishment; people succeed without lifting a finger, while others never seem to make a go of it, whatever they do, whatever gargantuan efforts they make. The believer recognizes that injustice will somehow be taken care of in the next life: the criminal and the sloth will pay their dues. This may be one way of dealing with earthly injustice, but, perhaps because I inherited my godfather's skepticism, I do not believe divine justice. One must live one's life here on earth.

Ivry Gitlis is a wonderful Israeli violinist, whose successful career started in Paris. In a competition (Concours International Long-

Thibaud) which he entered as a teenager, he was picked by the public, although not by the jury. His performances spoke to the hearts of his audience, and they responded with their hands. I cannot remember who actually won that competition, but I know it is Gitlis who has made the career. He had the talent and the touch, and possessed that special "something" to which audiences respond.

This may sound like too simplistic an explanation for why some people become international stars and others end up in the back rows of orchestras, convinced that they play better than the soloist on the podium in front of them, and sometimes bitter at the way the fates have dealt with them. I believe what I'm saying here to be the simple truth, and it is a lesson I constantly teach my students. It is perhaps the most useful advice I can give them, but is often one they do not hear.

*

I started teaching in the early days of my marriage, not for the money—I've always managed to support my family through playing—but because people kept asking me to give lessons. I taught almost anyone who came to me, including some very bad flutists. They were usually on government grants, and I was paid directly by the state. I never liked to ask the students themselves for money: a trait I'd inherited from my father, who never gave private lessons, and never accepted cash from pupils. During the war, he did give a few lessons to some musically inclined farmers, but it was always in exchange for food, not money.

I have the same dislike of private lessons that my father had. We always used to be taught in groups, and we played in front of our classmates, which meant we could exchange ideas with other students as well as with the teacher; it also gave us our first taste of playing in public. Private lessons remove that dimension: it becomes a duet between student and teacher. The exchange is limited, and, if the student is not very good, often becomes a one-way street. I am an extremely social person and dislike this form of communication. I find private lessons dull unless the student is already a very good musician.

Nevertheless, I continued to give private lessons for several years, until one day Françoise asked me why I was wasting my time.

"You don't enjoy it, you don't ask for money, and the students don't play very well," she said. How firmly her pretty brunette head rests on her shoulders! I've always been the one who has trouble saying no to things. Had it not been for Françoise, I'm sure I'd have spent from morning to night teaching, playing, recording; recording, teaching, playing.

"Yes, you're right," I was forced to admit. "But if a student showed up who turned out to be excellent, perhaps it would be worthwhile— I'd learn something, too."

After that, I gave up teaching at home, and if students insisted that I hear them play, I would invite them over for a half-hour consultation. I didn't need to charge them for this, because all I really did was listen and give my opinion. I would sometimes find the very finest of the Conservatory students in my living room, and our consultation might stretch on into the evening, for it is always interesting to play and talk music with a talented player. I would sometimes meet with enthusiastic but not very good performers, who believed they had the makings of a career. I felt it my duty to encourage them to continue playing, but as amateurs—and to give up the idea of becoming professional musicians. I told them how much I always enjoyed playing with amateur musicians: they make up an important and appreciative part of any audience. I am just not a good teacher for an amateur and also hate to see a less-talented person waste time, money and effort with disappointment the only recompense.

*

I met Aurèle Nicolet in Paris after the war, in 1946. He was a student of Marcel Moyse at the Paris Conservatory. (He is two years younger than I, which explains why he was still in the class.) Our ways of playing the flute are quite different, and that is why we love to make music together. His personality, his expertise on the flute and his musical convictions have always fascinated me. When we first met, I had been asked to be a soloist for a Bach concert with the Orchestre de la Société des Concerts du Conservatoire (which became, at the time of Charles Munch, l'Orchestre de Paris). The program was to include the Bach Suite in B minor and the Fourth Brandenburg Concerto, with the local concertmaster and "another flutist, other than the orchestral flutists" (because they thought they had to be my enemies—let us forget their names! . . .) playing solo parts. I asked Aurèle if he was free. He was, and became one more enemy to the orchestra's flutists! It was Nicolet's first concert in Paris, and I am very proud to have shared it with him. Since then we have played dozens of concerts in Europe, South America and Japan, as well as a recital in New York City. He is my "brother-in-flute" and we feel a deep love for each other.

Aurèle Nicolet is responsible for changing the old German flute school into a French one when he was appointed principal flute of the Berlin Philharmonic under both Fürtwangler and von Karajan. His career as a soloist has taken him all over the world.

*

It was after I had given up private lessons and before I became professor of flute at the Conservatory that a young Irishman called me. His name, he said, was James Galway, and he had come to Paris to study the flute. He wanted to take lessons with me. I explained that I didn't give private lessons, but that he was welcome to come and visit me on the Avenue Mozart so that I could hear him play.

Jimmy came about twice. He played for me, and I did little more than encourage him and comment briefly on his playing. I wouldn't call the advice I gave him that of a teacher to a pupil, because he was so good that he didn't need to study at the Conservatory. I was not surprised when he was named flute soloist of the Berlin Philharmonic. I was also not surprised when he decided to make a career on his own.

People have said that there is a tremendous rivalry between us, and that it is for this reason we don't play together. This is all the result of media hype. Our schedules simply have never coincided in a way to make a joint recital possible. We have been on the same musical cruises of the Mediterranean, and we have certainly played together in private. I always enjoyed going to Berlin when Jimmy was in the orchestra there, and as often as not we would have dinner together and play duets afterward as musical friends often do. For the past several years I have invited him to be on the jury of my tri-annual flute competition in Paris, but he has never had the time.

I am glad that Jimmy has been able to make a successful career as a solo flutist. The best way to prove the point I have always contended—that the flute is a worthy solo instrument that can attract an audience in the same way as a piano, violin or cello—is to have as many people as possible be highly successful playing it.

Over the years, I have had the pleasure of watching many young flutists—ones whom I have had the honor to advise—take to the stage all around the world. One sees flute concerts given everywhere today, and the names Ransom Wilson, András Adorján, Robert Stallman, Karl Kraber and many others have emerged as soloists. Some teachers are jealous of the success of their students; for me, it is the opposite. I am never more delighted than when a student develops a successful career. It warms my heart to see Philippe Pierlot, Shigenori Kudo, Patrick Gallois, Philippe Bernold, Andrea Griminelli, Catherine Cantin or Jean-Michel Tanguy—and many others—listed at the head of a program. And I couldn't be happier when I hear of concerts by Eugenia Zukerman, Paula Robison, Marya Martin, Linda Chesis, Carol Wincenc and Toshiko Khono. The more great soloists there are, ones like Julius Baker, Jimmy Galway, Aurèle Nicolet, William Bennett, Michel Debost, Alain Marion, Maxence Larrieu, Peter-Lukas Graf, Christian Larde and Samuel Baron, the better it is for the health of the Flute—with a capital F.

I met some of these young and now not-so-young men and women at the Paris Conservatory when I started teaching there in the sixties.

In order to get there, I had to go through a quite bizarre job application procedure.

A teaching post at the Paris Conservatory had to be competed for—not by a practical demonstration of musicianship, or even by evidence of teaching skills. It was a "paper" competition. All candidates were asked to send in a résumé listing their highest honors. Then they were expected to pay a courtesy visit to all of the twenty or so professors who were already teaching at the Conservatory. Personally, I thought this a waste of time, though the authorities implied that if I didn't make these visits, it was unlikely that I would be accepted as a teacher.

I sent my résumé, plus a copy, to the director of the Conservatory. I knew that my credentials were better than those of any other applicant, and I also knew that I just didn't have the time or the inclination to make the cap-in-hand rounds tradition required. It was a competition of titles, and by rights I knew I should win.

Many people did, in fact, vote against me, but nevertheless I was named professor of flute. Walking through those venerable halls where I had studied during the war and was now a teacher, it often seemed to me that the walls—or perhaps it was a few people with turned heads and turned-up noses—whispered "Hrumph! And he didn't even pay me a visit!" as I walked by.

I always used to say that whenever I get into my car when I'm in Paris, it automatically starts driving itself to one of two places: either the Opera or the Conservatory. I may often want to go in exactly the opposite direction, but the car frequently decides to go the way *it* wants to go. Hardly surprising: after all, I played in the pit at the Opera almost every night I was in Paris from 1955 to 1962, and, for twelve years after that, I taught at rue de Madrid. Françoise has often had to remind me that we *don't* have a performance to give or a class to teach, just a dinner to eat!

Teaching at the Conservatory was a pleasure for me because I gave master classes. Such classes create the true environment in which students can learn to excel. It mixes pedagogy with performance, teaches a student to attend to his own playing and be discriminatory about the playing of others. The teacher's role is to give an honest appraisal of what he hears and sees, and to correct his students' mistakes. For the most part, I had excellent students, ones with talent and determination. There were, of course, others who were not quite so brilliant but who worked extremely hard and have since made successful musical careers for themselves. A few—less than a handful in the years I taught at the Conservatory—had to be asked to leave the class. They weren't working, and whether they had talent or not, I felt it was unfair of them to take the place of a student who wanted to make the most of a Conservatory education. I was helped a lot by my assistant, Robert Heriché, and later by Alain Marion, one of my father's former students, a wonderful flutist and teacher who, with Michel Debost, is now one of the two professors of flute at the Paris Conservatory.

I like to think of my classes as big families. There was, naturally, competition among the students, but I always tried to make them appreciate the different qualities of their classmates, and I don't think there was ever real jealousy or damaging rivalry. Many of the students became my friends, and most of them have gone on to secure positions in orchestras all over the world.

The same is true for the classes I gave at the Académie Internationale d'Eté which, with Fernand Oubradous, I helped to found in Nice in the early sixties. It's no wonder that this incredible place, which held classes in music, art, and dance, became the Mecca for flute students worldwide. Who wouldn't want to play beautiful music by the blissful Mediterranean when the bougainvillea is in bloom?

I was one of a faculty of about fifteen, which included many of my dearest friends. Robert Veyron-Lacroix taught harpsichord, Alexandre Lagoya the guitar, and Lily Laskine, that remarkable harpist who had explained to me about life's experience enhancing our love for different composers, was there, too, as were many of my friends from the Baroque Ensemble and the Quintette à Vent.

We were indeed a happy family, surrounded by our numerous

delightful offspring. To begin with, I had about fifteen students in my class, but over the years the number grew. I had to get one assistant, and then, when the number of students reached over a hundred, I had to have another. At various times, my helpers have included Alain Marion, and András Adjorán.

The students lived in a little building above the main villa, and after breakfast they would walk down through the beautiful gardens for their lessons. On sunny days, these were generally held outdoors. On the first day of classes, I would listen to all the pupils. The ones who needed to work on their actual technique I would assign to a class taught by a colleague. I myself do not know if I am a good teacher or not. As far as teaching beginners the basic technique of playing the flute goes, I generally feel it is better for them to study with someone more patient than I. One talent I do have as a teacher is my ability to demonstrate how good flute playing should sound, and how students can profit from the techniques they have learned. I can certainly point out when students are making mistakes, but if they need to practice their basic skills, my classes are not for them. My teaching method—if it can be called a method at all—is too "impressionistic" for that kind of instruction.

The most important criteria for any teacher is honesty. It is necessary to say what you believe to be true about the way a student plays. For some people, Americans in particular, this is often a bitter pill to swallow. My classes were always planned so that each student would get a chance to play in front of the class. One day, a young American girl played for us. I stopped her before she'd finished more than a few measures.

"*Trop de* dada, too much dada, *trop de* dada!" I said. I often find that Americans use a kind of accent on the upbeat that is simply not correct. I tried to explain to this student that she was playing the *music* badly, not that she was a bad *musician*. She needed to work harder.

"My dear, the sound isn't good, the technique is faulty and what you just played sounded bad."

The girl was obviously flustered.

"No one has ever spoken to me like that before," she said, with tears in her eyes.

It was my turn to be flabbergasted. She had obvious problems, and I was sure her American professor must have noticed them at some stage.

"I'm not saying this to hurt you," I tried to explain. "How would it be if I were to say *'bravo, c'est magnifique!'* in front of the whole class, when they can hear as well as I can that you aren't playing very well? I would be lying to them and I would be lying to you, and who would gain by it?"

The student was too stunned to speak, so I answered myself.

"Nobody. It's not that I particularly want to upset you, but I have to be honest and say that you played badly. And I have to say it quickly, because it won't help you if I wait fifteen days and you've almost come to the end of your stay here before you find out. If I tell you now where I think you need work, you can start practicing right away. You've just got to get used to the idea that I speak the truth to my students."

The girl dried her tears and resigned herself to harder work and more honest criticism: it was all she could do, as I wasn't about to change my style of teaching. It is like those parents who seem afraid that by disciplining their offspring they will give them some kind of undesirable complex. This is rubbish! If you let them do what they want until they are fifteen or sixteen and *then* start saying "This isn't allowed," and "That isn't allowed"—that, in fact, everything they want to do isn't allowed—it's going to come as an even greater shock to them and will probably result in even greater problems.

Discipline, a tangible indication of the difference between right and wrong, must start early on. My father showed me the back of his hand when I misbehaved, and I did the same to my son, and neither of us is the worse for it. After a sharp reprimand, my father would always say, "Come here, and give me a kiss." I understood that the punishment had come from his heart, and was meant for my own good. The physical contact afterward—my father's embrace—was very important, and it is something I rarely see in the United States, where male family members barely even shake hands. For a Frenchman, a Latin, this is an impossible way to live.

*

Despite a few ruffled feathers, the Nice summer school has always been a remarkable learning experience for everyone involved. I returned there year after year until my schedule became too intense and I was forced to make different choices. When my house in Corsica was finished in 1969, I started to spend my summer holidays there. The experience of teaching in Nice, however, is one I would never have wanted to pass up. We all made music and dined together. We gave recitals in the wonderful Montebello gardens, and we ate magnificent meals in the restaurants dotting the Riviera corniches.

My teaching today is limited to the occasional master class, primarily in the United States. I am not sure of the value of these day-long events. What can a teacher tell a student in one day that will help his future? Nevertheless, the classes seem to be very popular, and I'm always being asked to hold them. I usually spend the first few minutes telling some anecdotes to warm up the audience, and then I ask the students some questions about where they come from and why they chose to play the flute. The classes remind me of a television program, but they are always given in the best of spirits, and I am always honest in my criticisms. Yes, sometimes there are a few tears, but what can I do?

16

Finale

con

Brio

AT THE BEGINNING OF January 1982, Slava Rostropovich invited me to play a four-day engagement—to include the Khachaturian Concerto—with the National Symphony Orchestra. I knew a party was being planned for me after the concert on January 7, and I think Slava chose the dates on purpose, as he wanted to celebrate my sixtieth birthday with me. In the twenty or more years I have known him, he has rarely wasted an opportunity for celebration. I will never forget the time he played Papa Haydn—costume and all!—at a benefit for Washington's National Symphony. The stage was filled with celebrated musicians, and Slava arrived to hand out the instruments.

"I come from the heavens, and I come to play with you," he said, as he emptied his sack of goodies. That night Isaac Stern played a trumpet and I ended up with a triangle. I've always thought that if Slava were not such a marvelous musician, he would have made a great actor.

For the January concert, though, I came prepared—and with my own instrument. (I haven't as yet made a transcription of the Khachaturian Concerto for triangle!) Many of my friends were in town for the occasion, my wife had flown over from Paris, and after the concert I expected to join more than a hundred people for a party at the Watergate Hotel. But first I had the Khachaturian to contend with: a difficult piece that requires intense concentration.

As I arrived onstage and took my position to the right of Slava's podium, a rousing salvo of applause greeted me. Slava raised his baton, and an ensemble of young flutists on the other side of the stage broke into "Happy Birthday!" The orchestra joined in and so did the audience. Everyone sang "Happy Birthday, Jean-Pierre!" I was incredibly moved. American audiences are so wonderfully warm and enthusiastic. I had to make an enormous effort to compose myself. One cannot play the Khachaturian Concerto with tears in one's eyes.

This was the first event in a year full of emotional memories. Everywhere I played in 1982 I was met with celebration after celebration. I cannot thank my audiences around the world enough for their loving welcomes and good wishes. From those very first concerts in tiny halls to my appearances at the Hollywood Bowl, I have always tried to give as much of myself as I can during every performance. I tell my students that there are no small concerts: every time you play, it has to be with the best and most of your ability, whether it be for three hundred or three thousand people. An artist's greatest reward is the love he receives from his audience, wherever they are.

During the birthday party after the Washington concert, my friend Bobby Finn presented me with a gigantic birthday book that is filled with messages and congratulations from over a hundred and fifty of my friends and students. The book rather resembles one of those magnificent volumes created by the monks of the Middle Ages. Bobby made it with such love, and I was very moved. To turn the pages and see the photographs, the drawings and the words of love is to relive my life.

There is a note from Pierre Barbizet that reminds me of Marseilles, the Lycée Thiers, and our predilection for Voltaire when we were both fourteen. Gaston Crunelle, my professor at the Paris Conservatory, and Marcel Moyse send their best wishes. The picture of Robert Veyron-Lacroix shows him attempting my part of our duo, the flute. John Steele Ritter reminds me of how I introduced him to sushi on one of our Far Eastern tours. Jindřich Feld takes me back to Prague by means of a little tune, the notes of which spell out my name. A letter from Milan Munclinger reminds me of our favorite music. The sunny faces of Danny Kaye and Zubin Mehta are captured in a photograph taken when we were all in Israel for a concert. Isaac Stern and his family are shown in the water near my villa in Sagone, Corsica. Henri Dutilleux sent a wonderful page including excerpts from his flute compositions, the last of which was a blank staff entitled "Concerto for Flute." At least, with this start, future flutists have some hope of a marvelous addition to the repertory. Because Henri takes such time and care composing, I will be too old to play it when it's finished, but if he completes it in time for the next generation, I will be happy.

Scores of my former students are in the book, too, as well as dozens of other friends. Woody Allen and Diane Keaton inscribed a photo from the scene from *Manhattan* where they are in the Museum of Natural History; Woody was kind enough to mention my name in the movie. There is a picture of the great chef and horn player Georges Barboteu taken in his kitchen preparing his famous langoustines. Jim Henson and the Muppets all send me their best, with a special "kissy-kissy" from Miss Piggy in memory of our uproarious duet. And it goes on: the pages are filled with images of a life full of music and friends.

I keep my birthday book alongside the shelves of films I have made throughout the years of family gatherings and musical cruises. Pictures—pictorial records—have always been very important to me. Don't forget, I'm a movie fanatic, one who used to spend as many nights as there are days in the week at the cinema before my engagement calendar started to fill up. In fact, since my early youth, when my father and mother bought me a kind of projector called the Cinèma Lapierre, I have collected images. When I was ten, I almost burnt the house down after the celluloid for this device ignited; I had to wait several years before my parents trusted me to experiment with film again. But from then on I have bought nearly every new type of movie camera as it has appeared on the market. The result is a wonderful library of filmed memories that help me relive many of the highlights of my past.

I'm very happy to say that the second major highlight of my sixtieth birthday year is safely captured on three hours of video film. There is a popular television program in France called *Le Grand Echiquier*, which is presented by Jacques Chancel, a well-loved and highly intelligent journalist who focuses on the arts. Chancel's program devotes an entire evening to a single artist, reuniting him in the studio with his friends and colleagues for talk and music making. He invited me to celebrate my birthday in just such a *This Is Your Life*.

If there are any themes that I have tried to emphasize more than others during my life, "friends and friendships" is one that rings out loud and clear. During *Le Grand Echiquier*, I had the pleasure of playing again with some of the people who have been important to me over the years. Barbizet was there, and Pierre Pierlot; Alexandre Lagoya and Claude Bolling, too. There was a chamber orchestra with whom to re-create some of my favorite pieces. But what lingers firmly in my mind is the duet I played with Lily Laskine, the last time I played with her before she retired. That television studio seemed a long way from the Dominican church in which we performed Mozart's Flute and Harp Concerto when I was sixteen years old; this time a fragile Lily—she was then in her eighties—brought back all the memories of the more than forty years we had known each other. And sharing the stage with us was Marielle Nordmann, one of Lily's protégées and, I don't think it would be wrong to say, her favorite student. Today, I play with Marielle throughout the world, often in the same places where Lily and I used to give recitals. Each time we take the stage together, I am reminded of the powerful legacy musicians share. When their teachers no longer have the strength to play, their students take over, perpetuating the sound and spirit of their mentors into the next generation. I have watched with joy as Marielle's strong, distinctive spirit has kept Lily's presence alive. I know that my father felt this way about his students, and I feel the same way about mine.

On the evening of my sixtieth anniversary concert with the Orchestre National de Paris at the Salle Pleyel, I joined, with considerable pride, four laureates I had taught at the Paris Conservatory: Philippe Pierlot, the son of Pierre Pierlot; Jean-Louis Beaumadier; Patrick Gallois; and Philippe Gauthier in the Concerto for Five Flutes by Boismortier. This concert was the culmination of a day-long broadcast produced by Radio France in honor of my birthday. I had been asked to choose the program myself and was interviewed about my life and my music. I also got a chance to listen to several of my own favorite recordings and those of my friends. And, that evening, I got a chance to play with them again.

In the middle of the concert, I was once again greeted with "Happy Birthday!" only this time it was not played by an orchestra of young flutists. Unbeknownst to me, sixty flutists, all of them friends and some of them my former students, were dotted around the hall. Under the direction of flutist Michel Debost, they got to their feet at the first bars of "Happy Birthday!" and played an arrangement composed specially for the occasion by Jean-Michel Damase. It was all very emotional. The problems I'd had tackling the Khachaturian Concerto in Washington seemed fairly minor as Isaac Stern and Slava Rostropovich joined me onstage for the Double Concerto for Violin and Cello by Brahms. It was a joy and an honor to conduct for such marvelous musicians. And then I put down the baton and took up my flute for a Telemann trio.

Nothing could have been more special! I was onstage with my dearest friends, many more were in the audience, and my family—including my father, who was still alive at the time—was seated in the front rows. Maybe if I'd practiced a little harder, Daddy, the concert would have been better. . . . But I cannot imagine how. It was a joyous coming together of a life in music—a life which I am glad to say is far from finished.

When I think back over my career, no one or two individual incidents stand out. I know I've had great successes as well as moments

that were less brilliant. But, thank goodness, my career is not yet
over. I always have the feeling that I'm just midway along in it, which
is perhaps overly optimistic at my age, but then I've always been
someone who looks ahead to the future rather than back at the past.
What I *have* done interests me a lot less than what I'm *going* to do.
I don't harbor regrets. I don't wish I were twenty years old again.
When I was twenty, the world was embroiled in war. I don't want
to be twenty-five again, either—though things had improved by then:
the war was over, and I had a beautiful young wife. I live for the
next event, the next journey, the next meal.

My mother always seemed and still seems to have regrets about
her life. She is constantly saying, if only I had done this; if only my
son had been a doctor; if only my husband had taken a little more
care of himself, perhaps he'd still be alive. My father wasn't like that.
He, too, like me, always thought of the future. Luckily, like another
French artist, "*Je ne regrette rien.*" I have no regrets. I think my mother
would have been upset whatever career I had chosen: it's just her
nature. She is a woman swamped by regrets. But, despite what seems
like a negative *idée fixe* about my career, my mother taught me
prudence—at least, she tried to; even if I am by nature pretty carefree,
little by little she managed to instill some sense into me. Manou (our
pet name for her) has one quality that outshines all others; it is
incalculable and irreplaceable: her enormous goodness of heart. Her
affection and absence of egocentrism are astounding. She would gladly
give her life for others, especially for her family. And that has no
price.

Touring and recording will keep me very active over the next few
years. My schedule had been expertly arranged by Brigitte Hohmann,
the most charming angel of an assistant without whom I would not
know where I am, where I'm supposed to be, where I've just come
from or what I'm supposed to do. Ulla Sulzberger manages my time
from the offices of Valmalete in Paris with efficiency and affection;
the adorable Agnes Eisenberger lovingly takes care of my engagements
in the United States, and Mary Lou Falcone handles my public re-
lations with amazing diplomatic style. I am incredibly lucky to have

a feeling of being in the middle of my family with my two managers, Annie de Valmalete in Paris and Colbert Artists Management in New York.

I have so much to look forward to that I have no thought of slowing down. When our combined schedules allow it, there are records to be made with Isaac and Slava; I'll also be recording some Mozart with the Israel Philharmonic under Zubin Mehta. I will be making tours of Japan, South America and Europe. And I will spend about three months a year in the United States. There are master classes to give and recitals to perform; old friends to visit and new friends to make. There's no way I can think of retiring just yet.

Indeed, I hope that I will have the chance for many more years to remain in my profession as a professional: not someone who counts on their name to fill auditoriums, and then plays badly. Unhappily, I have known people who, when they reach the end of their careers, lose their ability to play and yet continue to perform. Their family and friends, who should explain that the time has come for the performer to put away his instrument, fail to do so, and the public is often left with nothing but a disappointing memory of a favorite artist. I hope that when *my* time comes, when my talent diminishes, my wife and my close friends will be able to tell me the truth. I don't want to end up like some performers who, as we say in France, *sucrent les fraises*: sugar the strawberries—a rather charming image with which to describe a doddering musician who trembles his way through a performance with shaking hands.

One has to keep making progress as a musician if one is to continue at one's best. For me, nowadays, to make progress is to gain with age what one might have lost with youth. One's physical capabilities may diminish, but as long as expression, intelligence and maturity become stronger, one continues to progress. When my experience fails to make up for any lack in my technical skill, then I hope people will tell me that it is time for me to clean the flute for the last time. It would be better to do other things in the musical world than to disappoint the public that has been loyal and appreciative over the years. You must never make the audience pity you.

Sometimes I think I would like my life to end after a concert. You are very happy and excited, and everyone comes to congratulate you. In that happy and elated moment of contentment, you turn your head and—puff!—you die of a heart attack. Of course, it wouldn't be so wonderful for the people who are with you, but I can't think of a better way to go.

People say that in the moment before death you see your whole life pass before you. I hope such a thing won't happen to me any time soon, but sometimes, in a dream, I experience much the same kind of phenomenon: a fleeting glimpse of special memories. I'm thinking more of my life as a musician than of my day-to-day life. There are certain pieces of music I instinctively associate with some very special people:

Georges Thill singing "L'Air d'Alceste" from Gluck's opera. Pierre Barbizet playing some of Schumann's *Carnaval*. Maurice André, in the gleaming Roman amphitheater in Ephesus, playing a Tartini concerto. Robert Veyron-Lacroix and Schumann's second "Romance." Pierre Pierlot and the second movement of Albinoni's Oboe Concerto. Milan Munclinger and our Franz Benda Flute Concerto. Slava Rostropovich and a Haydn concerto. Luciano Pavarotti in *Il Trovatore*. Claudio Scimone, I Solisti Veneti and Vivaldi's Opus 10. Isaac Stern and the Beethoven Violin Concerto. Jacques Lancelot and the adagio movement of Mozart's Clarinet Concerto. The Franz Liszt Chamber Orchestra of Budapest playing a Handel concerto grosso. Placído Domingo in an aria from Meyebeer's *L'Africaine*. Marielle Nordmann and Mozart's Concerto for Flute and Harp. The twinkling notes in the high register of John Steele Ritter's piano. And Lily Laskine playing anything at all, for she always made her harp sing so beautifully . . .

I cannot envisage living without music. Even though I try to have a less hectic schedule, it seems to me that the months fill up in the same way they've always done. Perhaps it's with the best intentions that my managers, my friends and I try to think about cutting back, but up until now it hasn't happened.

I am rarely ill, but sometimes when my schedule gets too hectic and my entertaining too rich, I am forced to slow down. I wish this never happened, of course, but, like everyone else, I am subject to the laws of nature. A few days' rest will generally put things right. Sometimes when I arrive at a concert hall I feel tired; I don't want to go on. I get discouraged, and wish I had followed my mother's advice and become a doctor. I am alone, a long way from home, and my spirits are low. The feeling lasts just as long as it takes me to change and get onstage. As soon as I start to play, I am caught up in the music; the fatigue and self-pity vanish. To play music as if it were a duty is inconceivable. Nothing could be worse.

Cellist Leonard Rose quoted an old Jewish proverb in my sixtieth birthday book, one that suggested I continue blowing that "gas pipe" of mine until I was a hundred and twenty. I won't hold my breath on this one; I know that these days you can continue to play the flute for many years, but after a certain age—and I am not sure when it will be—I will have to stop. I do not want to be "sugaring the strawberries," or to die onstage like Molière, but I hope that until the day I die I will be able to continue with music to the very end. After all, music has been, and still is, one of my greatest loves.

JEAN-PIERRE RAMPAL was born sixty-seven years ago in Marseilles, France. Unanimously recognized as one of the greatest flutists of all time, he performs more than a hundred and twenty recitals and orchestral concerts a year, and is also one of the most recorded instrumentalists. Rampal is noted for his interpretations of music that ranges from the Baroque to the modern, with excursions into jazz, Japanese and Indian music. He has championed the cause of the flute by expanding its repertory: unearthing, reviving, adapting and premiering a multitude of works. During the past few years, Rampal has turned with increasing frequency to conducting.

Rampal has been awarded many honors from many countries, including the Danish Leonie Sonning Prize, the Grand Prix du Disque de Montreux for his complete discography, and the Edison Prize. He is an Officier de la Légion d'Honneur, Officier des Arts et Lettres, and Commandent de l'Ordre National du Mérite. He lives in Paris with his wife, Françoise.

DEBORAH WISE is a former correspondent for *Business Week*, who lives in Paris.